VICES & VIRTUES

Knowing, Accepting, and Improving Yourself

A Step-by-Step Guide
to Conquering Your Vices
and Harnessing Your Virtues

ALEJANDRO ORTEGA TRILLO

CAROLINA GAMBINI, TRANSLATOR

Liguori

Imprimi Potest:
Stephen T. Rehrauer, CSsR, Provincial
Denver Province, the Redemptorists

Published by Liguori Publications
Liguori, Missouri 63057

To order, visit Liguori.org or call 800-325-9521.

Copyright © 2015 Alejandro Ortega Trillo

All rights reserved. No part of this publication may be reproduced, stored in a retrieval system, or transmitted in any form or by any means—electronic, mechanical, photocopy, recording, or any other—except for brief quotations in printed reviews, without the prior written permission of Liguori Publications.

Cataloging-in-Publication Data is on file with the Library of Congress

p ISBN 978-0-7648-2608-5
e ISBN 978-0-7648-7041-5

Scripture texts in this work are taken from the *New American Bible,* revised edition © 2010, 1991, 1986, 1970 Confraternity of Christian Doctrine, Washington, D.C., and are used by permission of the copyright owner. All Rights Reserved. No part of the *New American Bible* may be reproduced in any form without permission in writing from the copyright owner.

Translated from the Spanish version of the book, *Vicios y Virtudes,* published by Libros Liguori.

Liguori Publications, a nonprofit corporation, is an apostolate of the Redemptorists. To learn more about the Redemptorists, visit Redemptorists.com.

Printed in the United States of America
19 18 17 16 15 / 5 4 3 2 1
First Edition

PROLOGUE

It is with deep gratitude that I write the prologue to this edition of *Vices and Virtues*. First and foremost, I am grateful to God, who has taken this book far beyond my expectations. I am also grateful to the readers. The number of positive comments this book has received and continues to receive never ceases to amaze me. This simple, concise, and step-by-step approach to an otherwise vast and complex topic has been a resource for many. I hope this English edition continues to provide the same help.

My intent has never been to provide an exhaustive treatment of vices and virtues. How could I? Vices and virtues have such an immense role in our life that it would be impossible to cover everything in any one book. Broader and more exhaustive treatises on the subject are available for those of you who are interested in diving even deeper into the topic. I offer this book to you as a simple tool that might be helpful for those of you who have just a basic understanding of the topics covered and want to learn more.

I would also like to add that I did not write this book from the vantage point of a virtuous life. Like anyone, I also fight the constant internal battle between vice and virtue. In some ways, this book is a sort of self-portrait. Given the countless testimonies, many others have seen themselves in it as well. I'm not surprised. We all come from the same dust.

A few months after this book was first published, I received the following e-mail from a reader named Martha:

Dear Fr. Alejandro:

I finished reading the first edition of your book during Christmas. I went on to buy fifteen more copies of the book to give to friends, relatives, and acquaintances who I thought might need it. I gave one copy to my brother. A little while back, he asked one of his employees to wait for him in the car while he went into the bank. The employee flipped through several pages of the book out of curiosity and ended up borrowing the book to finish it. That next Monday, the employee returned the book without saying much. A few days later, the employee's wife called the office asking my brother whether he had noticed any change in him. Truth be told, no. However, she went on to recount how they had been at the brink of a divorce, but after reading a book he had taken home that weekend, she had noticed profound changes. As a result, they both had decided to give each other a second chance.

I trust this will not be an isolated story. It is my hope that after reading this book, you will have your own story of change and that God will lead you to new opportunities.

Fr. Alejandro Ortega Trillo, LC

CONTENTS

INTRODUCTION

One of the greatest insights I have had about humanity I owe to Alexander Solzhenitsyn, the Russian novelist and advocate for political change. In his book *The Gulag Archipelago*, he remembers how, after suffering a beating during his imprisonment, he fantasized about taking vengeance. He imagined reversing the situation so his persecutors became his victims. He felt hate erupting internally, seething up from a dark and, until then, unknown source. He saw himself in his mind's eye, feeling exhilarated by exacting his revenge with extreme fury and cruelty. Then he reexamined his thoughts and became aware of a dreadful and astounding reality. The fine line that divides good from evil does not separate one person from another, the good people from the bad people. Instead, it divides our heart from one side to the other.

The human heart is a mixed bag of inconsistencies and contradictions. The Bible describes it harshly: "More tortuous than anything is the human heart, beyond remedy; who can understand it?" (Jeremiah 17:9). In fact, the organ itself seems a perfect metaphor for what happens in the moral and spiritual realm. The regular opposing movements of the heart's operation, systole and diastole, contraction and relaxation, reflect how moments of grandeur and misery, strength and weakness, kindness and malice, and generosity and selfishness alternate within a human being.

The image of a child with an angel on one shoulder and a devil on the other is not so far from the truth. Saint Paul lamented bitterly his unrelenting internal battles between his "old self" and his "new self," meaning between the tendencies of the flesh and those of the spirit.

Perhaps that is why the Bible says to us: "Is not life on earth a drudgery, its days like those of a hireling?" (Job 7:1). From our birth, there is a mysterious force that leads us toward wrongdoing. We have to take action if we want to be virtuous. When we are able to find peace, it can vanish with our first temptation, sign of anger, or impatience. The day when we will find absolute peace and spiritual serenity, true control over our instincts seems to be perpetually out of reach. Our darker inclinations and tendencies are always there, ready to fight us at every turn.

This book aims to be realistic. Rather than eradicating those dark tendencies completely and permanently, it suggests how to take advantage of them. In fact, this book stems from the conviction that our internal growth is developed through the art of learning how to benefit from our failings, faults, and frailties in order to foster virtues. To put it simply, having to struggle isn't so bad. It is the price we pay to achieve spiritual maturity. The fruit of that maturity is a kind of peace compatible with the internal struggle we face every day, a peace that comes from not giving in.

The book has been structured into three stages: Know Yourself, Accept Yourself, and Improve Yourself. The reason for this is obvious. If you don't know yourself, you are probably still living in a world of illusions. If you know yourself but haven't accepted yourself, you are living in a world of disillusionment. Finally, if you know and accept yourself but don't try to improve yourself, you are more likely to give into your vices or conform to the status quo.

On one occasion, Thales of Miletus, a Greek philosopher, was asked what the most difficult task is for humans. Without hesitation, he answered: "To know oneself." To know ourselves is an art. It calls for high doses of introspection, objectivity, and courage. It has been said that we each have four faces, or versions, of ourselves:

- First, what is known by us and others: our public face;
- Second, what only we know: our private face;
- Next, what others know and we do not: our concealed face;
- Finally, what is not known by us or other people, but by God alone, because this face is hidden in the enigma of God's persona: our unknown face.

If to know ourselves we must be introspective, then to accept ourselves we must be humble. Humility is the price we pay to have a solid foundation on which to build. If we do not consciously and sincerely accept who we are—and who we are not!—we will not be able to take a single step toward spiritual maturity. We will be hopelessly lost.

Accepting ourselves does not mean resigning ourselves to the way things are. Accepting ourselves means recognizing our deficiencies and improving on them, as well as growing our strengths to make the most of them. We become better in what is already good, whereas in what is bad we become, at the very least, less bad.

To improve or to become better is not the same as appearing better. Seeking only the appearance of improvement is insincere. Frankly, being better might imply, in many cases, looking worse, as in being more humble, more aware of our own limits, and more realistic. Pride is a Goliath we have to conquer in order to grow. It is not a coincidence the greatest men and women in history have been exceptionally humble, like Gandhi or Blessed Mother Teresa of Calcutta.

Improving ourselves is always gratifying. Although our nature is wounded by our vices and sins, it does not cease to demand that we strive to be better. That is why when we grow and overcome our failings and limitations, we feel the joy of having fulfilled a duty.

The first part of this book reviews our most common vices, or failings. Seeing ourselves in one or more of these vices will help us know ourselves better. The second part is an invitation to accept ourselves as we are, vices and all, with confidence and peace of mind. In the third part, we will review the virtues that oppose each of the vices with the purpose of guiding our inner selves toward self-improvement. As a conclusion, the last chapters present a step-by-step approach for devising a life plan, as well as a guide—the "vital ten"—for transforming our everyday activities into an environment that promotes virtue.

We know from experience how easily good intentions weaken. It is not enough to make decisions and say we will change. We cannot depend on our own strength alone. Jesus was not kidding when he said, "without me you can do nothing" (John 15:5). We need God. That is why if we expect any kind of change to come from reading this book, we must pray and humbly turn to God. Only he will give us the light, wisdom, and strength to know ourselves with sincerity, accept ourselves with serenity, and improve ourselves with patience, realism, and determination.

Know Yourself

1. MORAL HABITS

As human beings we are, to a certain extent, the sum of our habits. A habit is a behavior that has taken root in our personality. When we repeat certain behaviors, they become part of who we are. That's why Aristotle defined a habit as a "second nature."

According to a study by Jim Loehr and Tony Schwartz, authors of the book *The Power of Full Engagement*, almost 90 percent of our daily activities are habitual. Habits are the autopilot of our lives. We shower, dress, prepare a cup of coffee, and drive to school or work by habit. These tasks require no more from us than minimal attention. This is a good thing! Our day would be exhausting if each one of our actions required complete concentration. Our habits allow for a balance between ease and agility in our daily lives.

At the same time, this state of autopilot can make habits dangerous. If we are not attentive, we can form harmful habits that can become damaging. Doing whatever we feel like is not always good, constructive, or beneficial. We have to show vigilance in validating good habits and purging the bad ones.

There are many different types of habits. Bodily habits have to do with things like our physical posture while standing, walking, sitting, or sleeping. These may have no more than orthopedic importance, but other bodily habits, such as facial expressions, are more relevant. No one is responsible for the natural beauty of their face, but we are responsible for the nature of our wrinkles. Warm and welcoming faces, as well as hostile ones, are forged in our hearts.

There are also mental habits, like our capacity to analyze and synthesize, to think in abstract or concrete ways, and to use inductive or deductive reasoning. These habits influence how we assimilate, process, and express knowledge, data, ideas, and so forth. The more developed these habits are, the greater our maturity and intellectual ability.

Although all these habits are important, the ones we are most concerned with here and the habits that form a foundation for our other habits are moral habits. Describing these habits as "moral" means we are dealing with habits that touch our essence as human beings. Morality is, in a way, the capacity a human has to be more, and also less, of a person. Unlike plants and animals, whose essence cannot grow or diminish, a human's essence is open to being perfected, as well as to being degraded. As the saying goes, "A tiger cannot change its stripes," but as humans we can change what we are. A tiger cannot become "detigerized," but we can dehumanize ourselves and others based on our moral habits.

Knowing and accepting this allows us to understand clearly what it means when we talk about vices and virtues. To talk about vices and virtues is to talk about moral habits that make us more or less humanized. A vice is a bad moral habit. A virtue is a good one.

Without a doubt, our vices and virtues shape us as human beings. They attest to our personal depth as well as to our human stature. When we speak of a virtuous person, we often refer to this individual as a "great man" or a "great woman." By calling the virtuous great, we are acknowledging their superior moral stature. However, when we speak of a person who injures, hurts, abuses, or kills people, we say: "How inhuman!" This is not because such persons cease to be human but because by their actions their human stature becomes diminished along with their moral stature. To speak of vices and virtues goes beyond certain pastimes or activities we are passionate about. A vice goes beyond smoking, coffee drinking, or card playing. Vices and virtues touch our very essence. That is why this book attempts, first and foremost, to be an invitation for each of us to become more of a person, that is, to grow as human beings and live up to the greatness of our true essence.

2. DESIGNED TO LOVE

The Happiness Paradox

Scientific evidence, paired with our understanding of our faith, shows that the slow evolution of the cosmos leading to the dawn of humankind on Earth has obeyed an "intelligent design." This creative intelligence has arranged everything so that the universe would be the dwelling of a privileged creature. Thus, we ourselves must be creatures of remarkable design and our design suggests our function and purpose.

As human beings, we have a particular design. Each of our components, each part of our body, every detail of our outward appearance speaks of a purpose. In philosophical terms, it speaks of our "teleology" (the purpose of our design), which is to love. Our eyes love and fall in love. Our hands caress, support, care for, and hold other hands. Our arms give refuge and offer unique tenderness. Our warmth invites affection and intimacy. As well, our inner nature is no less astounding. Sensitivity, sensibility, intelligence, will, and emotions equip our fine-tuned system with the ability to perceive, recognize, welcome, and experience love in its passionate impulses as well as in its subtlest stirrings.

This is not the full extent of human design. A human being's will tends, as by instinct, to pursue goodness and happiness. This instinctive yearning for happiness is at the core of all our actions. Deep down, the wicked are in search of the same thing as the saintly, but they pursue it through different actions that yield very different outcomes.

It is not easy to define happiness, but we can come close to understanding what makes us feel it. Happiness comes to many of us as the joy that comes from fulfilling an aspiration. The deeper this goal is entrenched in who we are, the more intense those feelings of happiness become. The greatest and most profound longing of all human beings, emerging from our design, is to love and be loved. Love is the only source of true happiness for us, and deep within ourselves, we know it.

Happiness does not exist outside of us. It is not found in fame, possessions, pleasure, or personal achievements. These are simply fleeting illusions of happiness, like a mirage in the desert. Many people have tried to find fulfillment in these illusions but end up feeling empty. In the search for happiness, they made the ultimate mistake, living for themselves. In so doing, their lives have lost all meaning. We can think of it like this: Those who do not use their life for good will not have a good life.

> I remember a man in his forties who came to me for advice. He was depressed and disillusioned with life. He was married and had three children but was currently separated from his wife and was now living alone. He was a successful businessman. He traveled extensively for work and made enough money to satisfy his every whim while still supporting his wife and children from afar. By all accounts, he should have been happy with his success and his lifestyle, but he still felt empty. I think it was God who inspired me to ask him, "Who do you live for?" Shaken, he answered, "That is such a good question." He buried his face in his hands, and in tears responded, "For no one!"

Even when we find ourselves in a situation like this businessman, happiness is not beyond our reach. We will find it when we unleash our capacity to love. Looking for happiness in and of itself is a mistake. Happiness seems so elusive because it is an effect, an outcome. Before we can find true happiness, we must first learn to love.

It's a difficult concept to understand, especially in a culture where we are told "you will be happy if you have…" and not "you will be happy if you do…" But in reality, happiness is like the tail of a dog. If a dog chases its tail, the dog is just going in circles, tail always out of reach. If, on the other hand, the dog ignores its tail and responds to its owner's call, happiness will follow it everywhere. This is another way of thinking about Matthew's Gospel paradox: "Whoever finds his life will lose it, and whoever loses his life for my sake will find it" (Matthew 10:39).

This is our original design, the intelligent design for which we were created. Only love reveals our innermost self, that from which and for which we were made. Only the person who loves knows how to live. Love is ultimate wisdom.

3. SELFISHNESS

Living With the Enemy

Life has never been easy. At times, everything goes wrong. The water in our shower is freezing; our kids are aggravating; traffic is maddening; the news, flat-out disturbing; and that black cloud of bad moods seems to linger overhead no matter what we try. These are the everyday enemies to serenity.

Yet none of these things compares to our own ego when we let it stay unrestrained, inflated, or hurt. Our ego magnifies that black cloud overhead. Leaving our ego unchecked makes all those everyday enemies even worse, because our ego makes everything about us. When our ego is kept in its place, daily hassles will not deprive us of anything more than what is truly necessary to resolve them.

The word "ego" comes from Latin and means "I," our "self." This explains why exaggerated selfishness is also called "egotism." Selfishness is an excessive eagerness to defend, protect, glorify, please, and indulge our own I, typically at everyone else's expense. In short, it is misguided self-love.

Genuine self-love exists. Acknowledging with joy and gratitude who we are and pursuing personal growth to become a better version of ourselves is not only legitimate self-love but also mandatory. We see this message in the well-known Gospel parable about talents. The servant who was given one talent (coin) hid it and gave it back to his master intact. He did not lose it or waste it, but he did not put it to use either. He failed to take his talent and make something of it, and because of that he was condemned (see Matthew 25:24–30).

Selfishness is deeply rooted in the human heart, the grim legacy of original sin, from womb to tomb. We know all about original sin from the Bible and its consequences for Adam and Eve, but we don't have to turn to the Bible to confirm its effects are still in our world today. From childhood on, we have all seen and indulged in some form of selfish behavior such as temper tantrums, possessiveness, and antisocial behavior. What mother has not endured at least one of these?

Given that we are designed for love, our entire being is allocentric, or oriented toward others. Selfishness opposes this most natural tendency. Some will claim that to love others, we have to love ourselves first. Even though to a certain extent this is true, I think we are only able to love ourselves to the extent that we find ourselves capable of loving others. Loving others constitutes our innermost essence. It's like a mirror for our hearts. To the same degree that we see ourselves loving others, we are able to know, value, and love ourselves. Those who do not love anyone are strangers to themselves, and, because of this, are unable to love themselves.

We all coexist with selfish and egotistical people. Perhaps they infuriate us or make us suffer. They may even make us physically ill! But sooner or later someone will enlighten us that we are like that too, as was the case for King David: "You are the man!" (2 Samuel 12:7).

You, I, and all human beings are selfish. We all have that defect in our hearts. Who has not, at some point, been frightened of him- or herself? Who has not done something terrible, perhaps in a moment of fleeting passion? Who has not had to weep and mourn an irreparable mistake?

Bishop Fulton Sheen, well-known during the 1950s for his TV show *Life Is Worth Living*, was invited to lead a spiritual retreat for prisoners at a maximum security prison. The renowned preacher certainly did not feel as if he was on his own turf. How should he address those inmates, the most innocent of whom was convicted of five murders? As the story goes, the good bishop began by saying: "The only difference between you and me is that you got caught and I didn't."

Selfishness is an intruder that remains with us and makes us suffer for as long as we let it have control. It is a serpent with many heads that haunts us constantly. Each vice and moral defect is one of those heads, threatening us with venomous fangs.

In other words, selfishness is the root of all vices. A vice is a destructive moral habit, a behavior ingrained in our way of being that harms us and those around us. Vices, like parasites on a tree, drain the soul's sap, desiccate the heart, and infest the best fruit and our most noble aspirations.

Unfortunately, selfishness cannot be eradicated completely. The parable of the weeds illustrates this situation with tremendous realism (see Matthew 13:24–30). When the servants ask their master if they should gather up the weeds, the answer is, "No, if you pull up the weeds you might uproot the wheat along with them" (Matthew 13:29). Next to the weeds there is also good wheat that thrives, perhaps in spite of the weeds, or even because of them. This is what happens with selfishness. The presence of malice always offers us the opportunity to stand out.

So while selfishness itself is not enough to prevent us from living a virtuous life, it still has to be resisted and subdued with utter resolve. The first step is to understand it better. We need to unmask it, size it up, recognize it, and even anticipate how it manifests in us so as to avoid an ambush in a moment of carelessness or weakness.

Selfishness should not scare us or hold us back. As dreadful as it may seem, selfishness is manageable when we face it with intelligence and determination supported by divine grace. Furthermore, our daily struggle against selfishness—as leadership expert Santiago Álvarez de Mon—says in his book *Desde la adversidad*—will awaken methods and resources in our personality that would otherwise remain undeveloped. In fact, selfishness could become our best sparring partner, making us quicker, sharper, and stronger when it comes to standing up to our vices.

4. SENSUALITY AND PRIDE

The Original Imbalance

As human beings, we are complex. Body and soul, genetics and upbringing, temperament and experience, nature and grace—all contribute to make us unique, original, unrepeatable, and unpredictable.

In the last chapter, we discussed how original sin brought about disarray. Original harmony became imbalance and tension. Love, that spontaneous impulse of the heart, became wounded and antagonized by an opposing force, selfishness.

Before long, selfishness bore its first and perhaps most bitter fruit, division. So from the beginning of time to today, humans have felt divided between selfishness and virtue, torn by painful wounds, in all of their dimensions. We rebelled against God, invented war against others, betrayed our own integrity, and along the way, destroyed the balance of creation.

We are not alone in our battle with selfishness, as Bible stories attest. Adam disobeyed God. Cain killed Abel. David succumbed to the desires of the flesh by committing adultery with Uriah's wife. Noah, who obeyed God, nevertheless was witness to the great universal flood that destroyed the world because of its unrelenting selfishness.

Humankind's internal divisions caused us to lose the harmony between body and soul, which remain unreconciled. Works of art and literature have described in detail that relentless struggle, of which the real battleground, bathed in blood and bitterness, has been our heart. Body and soul were left not only disjointed but also wounded by selfishness. The body was diseased with sensuality and the soul with pride. This was the origin of disordered passions. Few have expressed the drama of that internal battle as forcefully as St. Paul: "For I take delight in the law of God, in my inner self, but I see in my members another principle at war with the law of my mind, taking me captive to the law of sin that dwells in my members. Miserable one that I am! Who will deliver me from this mortal body?" (Romans 7:22–24).

The word "passion" has its roots in the Latin verb *patior*, which means "to endure," or "to suffer." Passions are spontaneous inclinations or tendencies that can be very intense. They are almost always awakened by a stimulus that strikes a person's senses, feelings, or even the person's higher faculties.

Passions are not either good or bad. It all depends on the direction and course passions are given. Some passionate people have the capacity to channel that passionate energy with such skill that they accomplish the extraordinary. Not long ago, a film brought the late Nelson Mandela (1918–2013), the celebrated former president of South Africa, back into the international spotlight. His tenacity and good sense marked the before and after of his country's history, deeply wounded by the racial policies of apartheid. Mandela's harrowing background—he spent twenty-seven years in prison because of his opposition to the regime in power—and his subsequent political triumph were the result of his deep and relentless passion for justice and a legitimate sense of pride, channeled toward an objective of great consequence for his people. He rightfully received the Nobel Peace Prize in 1993.

When referring to negative passions, we often think of sensuality and pride. A healthy sensuality or legitimate pride does not exist. These are essentially disordered passions, resulting in pain, suffering, turmoil, distress, and loss of peace, in addition to anxiety and anguish. By their very nature, these passions are transient. Sadly, it often happens that by the time such passions withdraw, the harm has already been done, causing an offensive word, a broken friendship, or an action with unfortunate consequences.

A woman once came to see me because, in a moment of passion, she had gravely insulted her husband. She wanted to make amends for the situation and ask for forgiveness. She had not meant what she said, and she knew the situation should have been handled differently. She felt that after this nothing would be the same, and perhaps it would not be. Cleaning up the damage left in the wake of our passions can be even more difficult than controlling our passion in the first place.

Sensuality and pride are underlying generic passions. They form the roots from which more specific passions sprout, like limbs from a tree trunk. If nurtured and assimilated into our daily behavior, these limbs become vices or moral flaws.

Sensuality is the root of laziness, intemperance, lust, excessive attachment to comforts, and greed. Pride incites arrogance, vanity, self-reliance, hypersensitivity, and rebelliousness. Each one of these vices will be the subject of its own chapter later in this book.

We are all afflicted to a certain degree by each of these vices. Each person, however, tends to lean more toward one of the two main categories of sensuality or pride, and within each category, a specific vice becomes that person's dominant flaw.

I have asked various groups of people: "If you could choose, by which root flaw would you rather be afflicted, knowing full well that both are harmful and that a tendency to one or another is inevitable?" Most choose vices related to sensuality.

These vices are physical in nature and are thereby more visible. So, even though such vices are more noticeable to others, they are also easier for us to see in ourselves and thus easier to confront. The enemy is visible. Vices stemming from pride, on the other hand, are spiritual in nature, which makes them more subtle, almost imperceptible. Consequently, vices related to pride are more difficult to identify and combat.

Regrettably, we cannot choose our passions in real life. Doing so would mean these cease to be what they are, passions. Instead, our passions arise spontaneously in each of us, given our particular temperament and predispositions. We must discover which passions are predominant in our personality, and in particular which is our dominant passion or flaw, in order to oppose it with intelligence and strength.

THE TREE OF VICES

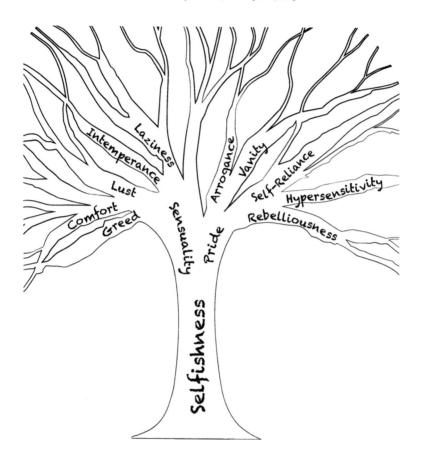

5. LAZINESS

An Unremarkable Life

Laziness is a worm that eats the substance out of our lives. It is the first offspring of sensuality. Laziness is defined as indifference, apathy, or negligence of our daily obligations. It can also be defined as sloth, neglect, or carelessness in our actions or activities. It is the defining characteristic of the "couch potato," the deadbeat, and the slacker. Without a doubt, it is a very familiar vice.

Despite its appearances, laziness is a life choice. Just as we can choose something pleasurable, we can also choose an attitude of indifference, apathy, or negligence. No one is coerced into it against their will. Some lazy people can be rude and crude, exuding their indifference. Others can be more refined, even sophisticated, and they practice their laziness in a socially acceptable way.

The lazy minimalists are ruled by the law of minimal effort. Anything they do or make—be it a product, service, or anything else—could be more complete, better quality, or more nicely finished, but is not. I have an eye for detail, and I always look for finishing touches. I am fortunate to have lived in several different countries and seen many cities. I have a habit of noticing the details of roads, curbs, and sidewalks, like how recently the lane dividers have been painted or whether or not the sidewalk is full of cracks and worn. There are huge differences between cities and even more so between countries. In theory, it requires the same materials, design, and work for each; however, the finishing touches are very different! Is it a matter of supervision? Perhaps. But to me, it's a matter of attitude and industriousness. Laziness can become a community, even cultural, issue, leaving its seal on the attitudes and behaviors of entire populations. It is the seal of neglect. The second type of lazy person is the messy one. This person is identified with disarray. I often wondered as a child what my mother meant when she came into my room, yelled with frustration, "This place is a pigsty!" and forced me to tidy it up. My mom may have gone overboard in her efforts for cleanliness, but I am still grateful she demanded it! Messiness can be as addictive as any other vice. Persons who are lazy make themselves believe that order is a characteristic of obsessive people, and they are not like that. Their desk, bedroom, office, time, and activities are subject to improvisation, and as a result, the random impulse of an unstructured personality.

The selectively lazy is a more peculiar type. This type of laziness is not a full lifestyle but instead focuses on certain areas, for example, the hard workers who refuse to do any kind of physical exercise. Others suffer from mental laziness. They diligently follow orders but are apathetic when it comes to thinking on their own. Additionally, some suffer from spiritual laziness and indifference, which is an attitude of negligence toward religious practice, prayer, or any other pious activity.

Possibly the most dismal type of lazy person is the inactive one. This person is constantly searching for opportunities to rest, so much so that the concept of time is lost. Life passes by in dullness and monotony. Inactivity eats away at even the best of the person's abilities. It is very likely that at the end of a seventy- or eighty-year journey through life, this individual will be surprised by how much, or really how little, has been accomplished.

The word "service" does not appear in the dictionary of the lazy person, because to serve, laziness must be stripped away. The lazy individual is almost "antiservice," not coming into this world to serve but to be served. In this way, the lazy lose the best opportunity for humans to love, which is through service to others. The consequences of such an attitude are devastating for everything but above all for marriage, the family, and other close relationships.

I recall a man who had been married for twenty years to an extraordinary but terribly disorganized woman. He was convinced he would have the perfect marriage if only his wife were more organized. He was exhausted from trying to explain his frustrations to her and constantly sorting out her messes. His wife's behavior was the cause of many disagreements in their marriage. There was nothing else I could suggest but that he overlook this flaw to keep the peace. His experiences led me to a sad conclusion. Almost always, where a lazy person lives there also lives a frustrated spouse.

Am I lazy?

- Do I live by the law of minimal effort?
- Am I disorganized with my time?
- Do I easily leave things for tomorrow and never go back to them?
- Are my desk, work table, drawers, and other personal items in disarray?
- Do I take care of my personal appearance?
- Am I negligent with my obligations?
- Do I find myself doing nothing more often than I'm engaged in activities?
- Do I dodge intellectual work?
- Do I feel apathetic about my spiritual life?

6. INTEMPERANCE

Everything to the Extreme

Aristotle referred to human beings as "rational animals." This is not a novel definition, but it does help us understand why advertisements aim so many messages and provocations at a certain undeniable part of our personality. The real potential customer is the animal we carry inside.

As humans, we are both physical and spiritual beings. As such, we cannot deny that we have innate ties to the physical world, even the animal kingdom. In fact, if you were to take a simplified view of humans from a purely scientific standpoint, it would be easy to think we are nothing more than animals. We are slightly more complex than some, but animals nonetheless.

That would not be the whole truth. We are different from animals in essential ways, and the distinction does not depend only on the presence of a spiritual soul. Our physical body is also different in that it is positively human. In fact, more than having a body, we are corporeal; more than instincts, we have tendencies; and although our ability to sense and perceive is fundamentally physical, it is also spiritual in a certain way.

Being corporeal means having needs and tendencies that manifest themselves in the form of sensual appetites. Thirst, hunger, and sexual impulses are appetites that reside in our physical body and fulfill functions essential to the survival of the individual as well as the species.

From this perspective, every appetite has a reason for being and is good in its own way. However, this dimension of ourselves has also been disordered by selfishness. Our senses have become inclined toward evil. That is to say, our sensual appetites are bent toward a disordered search for pleasure with regrettable and even fatal outcomes.

In classical antiquity, the Greeks distinguished between what was Apollonian and what was Dionysian, referring to the dichotomy between Apollo (god of sun) and Dionysus (god of wine, also known as Bacchus). Apollo was the god of order, moderation, and balance. Dionysus was the god of excess, including excesses in pride and arrogance, which the Greeks called "hubris." Even today, we all know the terrible strength and destructive power of hubris, which resides in the shadows of our sensuality. It's easy to feel weak in the face of those fierce tendencies, our senses that drag us along with the strength of five indomitable beasts.

When I turned eight years old, my father planned a party for me in our back yard. One of the games we played, a variation of tug-of-war, required us to find a partner and be tied back to back. The object of the game was to pull against each other and drag your opponent to your goal post, about ten feet away. When it came time to pick my opponent, I chose someone younger, but much bigger, than I. He may have only been seven years old, but he was built like a bull! It only took him seconds to drag me to his goal line. As my dad untied us he whispered in my ear, "Next time, choose more carefully."

Unfortunately, when it comes to our senses we have no choice. We have to brace ourselves and fight. When our senses and impulses push us toward harmful or inappropriate behaviors, we must do battle with restraint and control. When we lack control over our sensual appetites, it is called "intemperance." The more these appetites go unchecked, the more intemperate we are, the more our senses drag us along, and we become blind to the damage that is being done. An intemperate person ends up becoming both the victim and the slave of his or her senses.

One of the most well-known expressions of intemperance is gluttony, or excessive eating. Gluttony is a moral disorder and does not apply to those people who are compulsive eaters due to a psychological or medical disorder. We see gluttony in history when we read about feasts in the Roman Empire that would last for days. Those in attendance would vomit once full so they could continue eating. We might not see that exact type of excess today, but we do see other excesses such as spending exorbitant amounts of money on the smallest delicacy or a voracious intake of junk food. Some people are only deterred by seeing threatening numbers when they weigh themselves. Others have lost all restraint and given themselves over entirely to obesity with all its unfortunate consequences for their health. Obesity, we should mention, has become the most unpunished serial killer of our times.

Another way in which intemperance commonly manifests itself is through alcohol abuse. There are degrees of abuse from occasional intoxication to outright alcoholism. It is difficult to determine the actual roots of alcoholism. Some research points to a hereditary predisposition combined with upbringing and social pressures, which is seen especially in young adults. In some cases, alcohol starts as a temporary relief to stresses and hardships before becoming a hardship itself. As this behavior worsens, the addiction to alcohol goes from being psychological to physiological, resulting in a physical need. At that point, willpower, no matter how strong, is not enough. One must seek professional help and the assistance of a support group.

The use of illegal drugs is another manifestation of intemperance. In the case of some narcotics, intemperance is aided by the substance itself. Some narcotics can become instantly addictive, and even if used only once a dangerous new addiction can be born. As with alcohol, there is a psychological and physiological dependency that willpower alone is not enough to stop.

There is one more manifestation of intemperance, which if left unchecked evolves into the vice discussed in the next chapter. This form of intemperance is called the "wandering eye." Out of curiosity or simply a distracted gaze, our eyes tend to wander everywhere. In today's world, brimming with suggestive fashion and erotically charged advertisements, it takes mere seconds to find something that excites our senses. A wandering eye can vary in intensity, from the brief consent we give ourselves for a casual glance, to consciously and consistently relishing lewd stares when we come across images such as a woman in tight or revealing clothing, a suggestive image on the internet, or an erotic scene at the movies or on television.

The consequences of intemperance are well-known and, in many cases, catastrophic. The more an individual allows sensual appetites to take control, the more his or her intelligence becomes muddled and the will weakened. Such persons become a pawn in the hands of their senses, slowly consumed by vices that sicken body, mind, and soul.

The damages caused by intemperance go well beyond the individual. His or her spouse, children, and friends all suffer from the intemperate person's failings. They all get frustrated. They all lose their patience. The fallout that results from intemperance gives clear evidence that we carry our own worst enemy inside us.

Am I intemperate?

- Do I wander through life trying to capture any and every sensation that brings me pleasure?

- Do I have a wandering eye? Do I fall prey to exploring what may not be appropriate?

- Do I easily give in to indulgences even if I know they are not good for me?

- Do I give in to gluttony?

- Do I knowingly eat foods that are bad for me without moderation?

- Do I turn to alcohol when it feels like I am losing control?

- Do I use drugs?

7. LUST

A Slave to the Eros

Today's media and pop culture is filled with erotic pollution. Movies, television, print media, and the internet have given us an unprecedented number of resources at the service of the flesh. In today's world, surfing freely through the internet is comparable to wandering through the red light district of a major city. Even just walking in our neighborhoods, we can run into salacious scenes including strip clubs, adult stores, and other centers of an erotic nature, not to mention sexually charged advertisements that have nothing to do with adult entertainment.

In any event, this sexual barrage would not have an audience if we did not carry a selfish proclivity toward sexual pleasure, lust. The adult-entertainment industry has been and will continue to thrive as long as this disordered passion continues to ignite the flesh of men and women of all ages and backgrounds. Everyone is a potential client.

Lustful actions do not include what may occur involuntarily, like a fleeting and involuntary thought, an unexpected sight, or even an unwanted physical arousal. A lustful action is the conscious and deliberate pursuit and gratification of sexual desire outside of marriage. Even within marriage, lust can be found if those desires have become disordered and God has been pushed out of the center of the marriage. Lust takes on many forms, from procuring one's own solitary sexual pleasure (masturbating) to sexual relations outside of marriage.

A substantial number of people in today's society view these acts as normal and abstaining from them as old-fashioned. They see masturbation as a normal way to release sexual impulses. This habit contradicts the purpose of sexuality. Isn't our sexuality designed, even physically, for the mutual self-giving of a man and a woman? To exercise this capacity alone ends up being a contradictory act.

A 19-year-old young woman asked me recently why these acts are considered morally wrong: "Aren't these natural appetites? Why is it wrong to satisfy them?" The young woman, who had a boyfriend and was considering having an active sexual life with him, was asking why sexual relations outside of marriage were not accepted within Christian morality, when these can be the fruit of genuine love. Perhaps many young people have intimate relations to release pent-up sexual energy, but others, like this young woman, want to express legitimate affection. "We wouldn't just be using each other for sex. It would be for love," she insisted.

There was honesty and a certain amount of frustration in her eyes. I invited her to reflect, explaining: "The gift of intimacy is such a beautiful treasure that it calls for the context of mutual and ultimate commitment." We can only find this context in marriage, in which a complete and lifelong commitment grants the couple the degree of devotion required for such a precious act. Outside of marriage, there is no degree of personal relationship, no matter how intense or sincere, that offers a sufficiently stable and committed framework for a sexual relationship.

In other words, sexual relations outside of marriage contradict the inherent value of sexuality. Sexuality is wonderful.

Its beauty and dignity are such that it deserves to be defended and protected from anything that may distort or cheapen it. As the Gospel teaches us, "Do not...throw your pearls before swine" (Matthew 7:6).

When sexual relations occur between two people and at least one of them is already married to someone else, the lustful offense is aggravated by infidelity and adultery, the consequences of which are well-known. Everyone suffers: the unfaithful spouse as a result of the shame and sorrow of having failed, and the victimized spouse from the pain of betrayal. Even when there is forgiveness, it can be difficult to trust again.

Another form of lust can be found in pornography. It is almost impossible in this day and age to avoid sensual images on billboards, movies, television programs, newspapers, and magazines. Pornography is an industry that is growing exponentially, and even if we don't bring it intentionally, it finds a way into homes, offices, and places of leisure. The degree of consumption varies from the person with a wandering eye who takes in everything within view to the person who pays per view for adult content and seeks it out explicitly, which can be a sign of addiction.

Recent studies have confirmed that pornography has psychological and emotional effects similar to alcohol and drug addiction. Individuals addicted to pornography disengage easily from their obligations and neglect their connection with others. Their vice isolates them in a sort of sexual confinement.

I will never forget a college classmate who suffered bitterly for having been caught up by this vice. He felt anxious, vulnerable, and deeply disappointed in himself. He longed to instantly erase the stain so many images had left in his memory, images that now disturbed and tortured him, but he could not. Pornography was taking its toll.

A common sign of a lustful person lies in perceiving every new temptation as a unique opportunity that cannot be missed. This individual is shortsighted, a slave to instant gratification who lives exclusively for the here and now and does not know how to wait. This is why those with impulsive and impatient temperaments are more susceptible to this vice.

Lust devastates many lives. Like a destructive tsunami, it leaves a grievous wake of hurt children, teen mothers, careers cut short, broken families, and a myriad of diseased people. There is massive social outcry against the effects of lust, but not yet against the pervasive display of permissiveness and eroticism that are the most frequent causes. As long as the world continues to be eroticized, we will continue to have the same results and many, many tears.

Am I Lustful?

- Do I knowingly let my eyes stray when presented with sensual provocations?
- Do I find racy conversations, secrets, or jokes amusing?
- Do I foster sensual thoughts or notions freely?
- Have I ever paid to watch pornography?
- Is masturbating a habit I'm unable to break?
- Do I allow passion to prevail over love in the way I treat my fiancé (fiancée)?
- If I am married, have I been unfaithful in thoughts, feelings, or actions?
- Do I seek out any opportunity to satisfy my sexual appetite?

8. COMFORT

The Bonds of Ease

In contrast to the devastating and painful poverty that can be found in a great part of the world, many people live in a society of comfort. Industry outdoes itself each day in producing new products to mitigate every conceivable inconvenience. Perhaps today's trademark is the triumph of automation over manual labor, with everything we need available to us with just the click of a button.

The quest for moderate comfort or ease is not a vice, but the excessive desire for ease or desiring comfort above all else turns it into one. Wanting this kind of comfort is an uncontrolled and selfish tendency and an offshoot of sensuality. This desire for a life of comfort and ease presents itself in different ways, depending on our lifestyle, but its symptoms are more or less the same for everyone.

The excessive desire for comfort is not to be confused with laziness. In fact, the comfort-obsessed person tends to be a hard worker in order to afford the luxuries that provide this desired lifestyle. Laziness lends itself to passivity, whereas the urge for comfort lends itself to activity.

The comfort seeker is fastidious, dodging anything rough or bothersome. Such a person gets irritated with inclement weather, financial shortfalls, any kind of discomfort, and cannot stand improvising. This individual cannot tolerate a cold shower. Sleeping on the floor instead of a plush mattress could be his or her worst nightmare. While traveling, the comfort seeker would sooner forget a spouse than a pillow.

The comfort obsessed does not like camping or outdoor adventures, preferring the peaceful calm of home to getting to know the outside world, and feeling more at ease in slippers than in hiking boots. If wealthy, this person seeks out five-star hotels with gourmet cuisine.

The excessive quest for comfort can spill over into other domains. It leads to seeking ease not just at home but also at work, only doing pleasant tasks and assignments that do not require any sacrifice. The comfort seeker has a plush office chair, removing his or her shoes whenever possible. Ergonomics is the favorite science. The comfort seeker avoids working late and any meeting or gathering that might be unpleasant or require taking on additional responsibilities.

In faith, the comfort seeker takes a low-key approach, avoiding commitment. He or she does not sign up for local missionary activities or humanitarian projects, staying away from those outings to avoid the hard work of such endeavors.

Inadvertently, the comfort seeker clips his or her own wings. This person limits the range and scope of activities, approaching life in a narrow way so as to not incur risks. He or she will never know the pleasure of breaking a record, conquering a summit, or of discovering new shortcuts. The comfort seeker's life is bound to a routine, to a listless and grey way of doing things, without surprises or adrenaline, but also without fun or happiness. Forgotten by this person is a basic principle of self-improvement: "Face your fears."

 I first learned the benefits of facing your fears, even if it causes momentary discomfort, from a man around fifty years old who asked himself what it was he feared most. The answer: "To go paragliding." (Paragliding is a sport similar to parachuting, where you jump off into the air from a high elevation and glide down with the aid of a parachute.) This man was determined to mark his fiftieth birthday by finally conquering that fear. He gathered all his courage and signed himself up for a daylong course to learn the technique and then jump. Although he knew the first jump would be done with an instructor, his legs still trembled as he walked up the stairs toward the training room.

Finally, the moment arrived for him to go up the mountain and head toward a cliff that opened up into a vast and imposing valley. This was the site where his flight would begin. The training had given him some confidence but had not completely banished his anxiety. When he finally made the jump, he was able to revel in the new and breathtaking experience. When his children and friends asked how it felt, he answered, "The fear I felt before jumping was the size of King Kong. Now it's only the size of a gorilla—a robust adult gorilla."

Many comfort seekers never bother conquering their fears. They just avoid them. If they have families, this attitude trickles down into the opportunities they allow for their children. In a certain way, they pass on their own insecurity to their offspring, limiting them to activities that are strictly under their control, with no chance for unpleasantness or anxiety. Their desire for comfort becomes a chain that immobilizes the entire family.

A comfort-seeking individual suffers when it becomes necessary to adapt to changing circumstances. Life is a patchwork of unforeseen events, some of which are harsh and burdensome. That is why, far from living at peace, the comfort seeker roams through life concerned by the array of possibilities that at any given moment might steal his or her comfort and life of ease.

Last, comfort seekers show very little solidarity with others. They look after their own comfort and ignore everyone else. It is sad to see them curled up in their own shells, like hermit crabs, not having the courage or willingness to grant others their space and suffer in the place of someone else. Solidarity requires us to forget ourselves and be part of a community, but comfort seekers are not willing to sacrifice their own comfort for anyone. They are not aware that happiness and stability can be found when we surround ourselves with a reliable community, so they go without.

We have all heard stories of heroism in which people have suffered great hardships to help someone. In particular, I recall the story of a young Jewish woman who, newly released from a Nazi concentration camp at the end of the Second World War, did not have the strength to walk to a train station. A very frail young man, nearly as weak as she was, took her in his arms and, with enormous effort and sacrifice, carried her to the station. Then, he somehow found a piece of bread and a cup of coffee for her. The young woman could not believe her eyes. It was the first time in a very long time she had held a hot beverage. Soon after, the young man disappeared. Years later, she learned that her caring protector had been a Polish, Catholic seminarian named Karol, who would later become Pope St. John Paul II.

Am I a comfort seeker?

- Do I consistently run away from any discomfort?

- Do I get irritated by harsh weather, such as rain, cold, or excessive heat?

- Do I have special needs to ensure my personal comfort, or would others describe me as overly picky?

- Do I avoid camping outdoors because it would deprive me of the comforts of home?

- Do I always avoid social or religious commitments that require substantial time or effort?

- Do I usually restrict the options for my family's entertainment or relaxation, which allows me to keep everything under control?

- Have I avoided helping someone in order to protect my own comfort?

9. GREED

The Riches That Impoverish

Greed is the disordered desire to acquire material goods. It refers to an unhealthy enjoyment of possessing and hoarding goods of all sorts. We must not confuse greed with the legitimate effort to acquire what is necessary to lead a dignified life or to amass the necessary resources to ensure an individual's or a family's financial security. Furthermore, greed cannot be diagnosed simply by the number of possessions or the cost of those possessions. A person can be financially secure without being greedy.

Greed, like all other vices, is a form of selfishness. Those who are greedy think only of themselves, of quenching their thirst to possess more and more. They are unable to see beyond their own "stuff" and scheme to possess even more. Other people's needs go unnoticed.

Depending on personal preference, it is possible to covet anything: houses, cars, jewels, clothing, accessories, stamps, tin soldiers, rocks, even cash. How paper bills can possibly excite the senses I don't know, but the greedy person delights in looking at and caressing those bills—or credit cards—as if they were truly pleasing objects in and of themselves.

Greed enters through our eyes. The greedy person believes all that glitters really is gold and must have one of everything lavish, interesting, attractive, new, and unique. He or she is more than willing to pay any price as long as the object is truly pleasing and impressive. The greedy person is willing to pay outrageous prices because of a longing to simply possess something valuable.

Once greed has entered through our eyes, it takes hold of our heart. It is our heart that forms attachments to things. Some people compare the human heart to a tuberous root, like a potato. Hearts spread roots in every direction. The greedy heart stretches its multiple and lengthy tentacles to grasp and hoard everything in its reach. Once the object of its desire has been procured, it has great difficulty letting go, while simultaneously wanting to procure something else.

Greed, like any other vice, harms. It is like an addiction, because the more the greedy person relies on a drug of choice, the more it is craved. Those who are greedy are never happy with what they have and can never be satisfied: "Where there are great riches, there are also many to devour them. Of what use are they to the owner except as a feast for the eyes alone?" (Ecclesiastes 5:10). They can ruin themselves in their incessant quest to get what they do not need.

The greedy person is a slave. Rather than owning material things, he or she is owned by them. This individual's heart is attached to material things to such an extent that freedom of spirit is lost. The internal attachment is an affective one that projects externally as an effective one. A greedy person cannot share possessions, having hands that only know how to be tight-fisted. In this manner, the greedy person is deprived of one of the greatest pleasures in life, which is sharing with love.

Greedy people are also showoffs. In this way, they become almost vain about their possessions. They are somewhat different from vain persons because they want to show off their possessions and not a projected image of themselves, but the results are similar. Greed leads nowhere. As greedy people focus their vital energy on owning more and more things, they neglect other essential aspects of their lives. In fact, the richer they become in material wealth, the poorer they become as persons.

We have all heard the tale of King Midas. He grew up obsessed with riches, especially gold. The king was eventually granted his greatest wish, which was that everything he touched would turn into gold. He was very pleased until he needed to drink, eat, and sleep. Everything turned into gold. Even the members of his court were turned from living beings into pure, hard, cold gold.

Greediness creates a paradox. Even when the greedy person has everything he or she could want, this person feels empty. Sooner or later, the greedy person realizes that nothing will be able to satisfy his or her desire for more and more. The truth is that nothing material, no matter how much you have, can fill your heart. The human heart longs for meaning and purpose that material possessions cannot give.

Am I greedy?

- Do I feel unsatisfied with what I have?
- Do I easily envy or covet other people's possessions?
- Am I a compulsive shopper?
- Do I collect clothing, shoes, jewels, and other accessories beyond what I need?
- Do I delight in counting and recounting all of my possessions?
- Do I obsessively collect particular material objects?
- Am I willing to pay a fortune for a one-of-a-kind piece?
- Do I feel fulfilled when I show off my possessions?
- Am I stingy? Do I rarely share or donate my belongings?

10. ARROGANCE

A Way to Earn People's Disdain

Now that we have covered the primary vices rooted in sensuality, we will move on to those rooted in pride. These include arrogance, vanity, self-sufficiency, hypersensitivity, and rebelliousness. We will discuss each one in detail in the following chapters.

Arrogance stems from excessive self-esteem. It is to believe, feel, or act superior to everyone else. The distinctive nature of arrogance relates to a misunderstood and, above all, badly channeled sense of superiority. The philosopher Benedict de Spinoza defined arrogance as the pleasure felt by those who think too highly of themselves.

Arrogance does not mean when we objectively and humbly recognize our own talents or when we feel accomplished and happy about reaching a goal in life. It is not arrogant to lead if that leadership is sincere. The true leader, although rising in stature above the rest, exercises his or her talent with an attitude of service. In fact, it is right to think of authority as service. Someone must lead, coordinate, or guide a family, work team, enterprise, or government for things to function.

In his book *The One Minute Manager*, Kenneth Blanchard makes use of an interesting image, that of a minute on the face of a watch. He explains that the purpose of this image is to remind us that we must dedicate a minute each day to look into the faces of people who surround us, whether at home or work, to remember that they are what matters most.

Arrogant persons, on the contrary, enslave, overrun, and oppress when exercising their authority. They are not considerate of the people with whom they live, let alone those beyond their immediate circle. At work and at home, they unhesitatingly demand and command tasks that could require unnecessary loss of sleep and unreasonable effort. They set arbitrary deadlines without any consideration of what others may have to endure in order to meet them.

Those who are arrogant are impatient, intolerant, and unsympathetic with regard to the limitations and deficiencies of others. *Everybody should be perfect, like them!* They are usually very harsh and critical, even if they keep it to themselves. They observe and are quick to recognize other's weaknesses. Surprisingly, they do not have that same keenness to recognize other's strengths.

An arrogant person has little to no empathy. This individual does not understand other people's feelings, moods, or points of view. It is a given that things should be done this person's way, according to his or her criteria. People surrounding an arrogant person, including his or her spouse and children, should function as smoothly as a machine, or better.

The arrogant person's golden rule is to demand not to dialogue or motivate. Those who are arrogant do not realize, as explained by Salvador Alva, "rigidness is good in stones but not human beings." Consequently, it's not uncommon to find their work teams with sky-high turnovers and rock-bottom loyalties. They fail to recognize this attitude until someone with a large dose of courage and audacity tells them. If their heart is in the right place, they will listen and rectify their behavior. Usually though, arrogant persons believe that others exaggerate. "If it's a hard task for them, it is due to my high expectations," they tell themselves. The arrogant only see their own goals. To reach them, they will run over anyone in their way.

Each arrogant person is a steamroller focused on personal ambition, and by virtue of his or her ruthless ego, leaves behind abused, wounded, and disheartened people.

To deal with an arrogant person on a daily basis is an absolute nightmare. The bullying style, hurtful words, and contemptuous attitude exasperate anyone in his or her path. Some react with resigned submission, perhaps with some hidden spite, but others, who are more courageous, rebel.

The Bible presents us with the enlightening account of King Rehoboam, son of Solomon. When he ascended the throne, he sought advice from the town's elders as to how he should govern. The answer was a wise one: "If today you become the servant of this people and serve them, and give them a favorable answer, they will be your servants forever" (1 Kings 12:7). However, Rehoboam did not take their advice. He chose to follow his younger friends' advice instead. "He said to them, 'What answer do you advise that we should give this people, who have told me, "Lighten the yoke your father imposed on us"?' The young men who had grown up with him replied, 'This is what you must say to this people who have told you, "Your father made our yoke heavy; you lighten it for us." You must say, "My little finger is thicker than my father's loins. My father put a heavy yoke on you, but I will make it heavier. My father beat you with whips, but I will beat you with scorpions"' (1 Kings 12:9–11). As a result, King Rehoboam soon had a rebellion on his hands, forcing him to flee the kingdom of Israel to seek refuge in Jerusalem.

Many prideful people find themselves at a sad end, in a forgotten and lonesome old age, as retribution for their tyrannical ways by those who were closest to them. Maybe that is the reason Benjamin Franklin asserted, "Pride that dines on vanity sups on contempt."

Am I arrogant?

- Do I think excessively well of myself, my talents, abilities, and judgment?

- Do I exercise authority by oppressing, bullying, and hurting others?

- Am I overbearing and inconsiderate with others?

- Am I impatient, intolerant, or lacking in understanding with regard to others' limitations or inadequacies?

- Am I dominating or rigid when expressing my personal opinions?

- Do I internally judge and criticize others' behaviors?

- Do I choose to demand instead of motivating?

- Am I like a slave driver?

- Am I proud of being thought of as harsh?

11. VANITY

Enhancing Your Image

Vanity is an illusion. It is born from an excessive desire to be praised and flattered. The great French author Gustave Flaubert said, "Pride is a wild beast which lives in caves and roams the desert; Vanity, on the other hand, is a parrot which hops from branch to branch and chatters away in full view."

The essential characteristic of vanity is cultivating and embellishing one's image in front of others with excessive care. The vain person has an obsessive need to look good, to make a good impression. There are two types of vain people: the one who has something to boast about and the one who does not. In the first case, the vain person will be pretentious and ostentatious, while in the second case, the vain person will paradoxically become inhibited, shy, and burdened by an inferiority complex.

Among people of the first group, the prevailing form of vanity is physical. In this case, they scrupulously tend to their personal grooming, check themselves in every mirror, show off their appearance, and flaunt their best attributes. A good indicator of this vice is the amount of time, pain, and money they are willing to invest in improving their physical image. Today, it is said that there is no such thing as an ugly person, just a poor person.

Another type of vanity is the intellectual type. In this case, the vain person never misses an opportunity to dazzle others by bragging about his or her intelligence and knowledge. Such know-it-alls always have something to say, an opinion to give, or a judgment or dogma to impose while calling attention to themselves. Perhaps we may be able to recall a certain classmate from high school or college who would raise his or her hand not to contribute to the discussion but to make a comment with the intent of letting others know he or she had a superior understanding of the topic.

Material vanity, perhaps more common among the nouveau riche, is expressed by displaying the most expensive designer wear, jewels, trips, cars, houses, and so on. In this case, the vain person feels as rich as King Solomon. Such a person cannot tolerate anyone competing with him or her in the lavishness of clothing, parties, houses, and more. Not that Solomon himself had that attitude. In fact, Solomon, having been given more riches than any other king before or after him, was a profoundly humble man by virtue of his wisdom. But when there is excess money and no wisdom to spare, there is a barrage of ostentation that, far from building a good reputation, leads to a bad one.

As mentioned earlier, there is another group of vain people, those who have nothing to boast about. This kind of vain person may be homely, mediocre, or untalented, but still vain. Such vanity makes him or her insecure, stiff, and shy. Not all timid people are timid due to vanity, but it is not unusual to see vanity displayed through shyness and bashfulness. Such vain persons fear nothing more than making a bad impression, thus going out of their way to avoid making an impression at all. They keep to themselves, hiding in seclusion to avoid the danger of their weaknesses being exposed. Their mantra is, "Better dead than ridiculed!"

Throughout my early years in the seminary, I was very nervous any time I had to read in public. I would become short of breath and was unable to finish full sentences. I experienced first-hand the vicious cycle of insecurity. The fear of being made fun of made me insecure, and those feelings of insecurity fed my fear, creating a downward spiral that ended with a total mental block any time the task of reading in public came to me. Finally, one of my mentors discussed this with me, telling me it wasn't the reading that was the problem but actually my fear that was coming from feelings of vanity. It was only when I overcame my fear of being ridiculed, which took a few years, that the insecurity ceased, and with it, my nervousness. I learned the importance of appearing ridiculous every now and then.

The opposite symptom of vanity is the addiction to being applauded, recognized, and praised. This kind of recognition works almost like a recreational drug, particularly for insecure people. Vain people will do anything for praise and recognition, even using sophisticated forms of manipulation, although not always consciously. They are often flattering and obsequious, bending over backward to be liked and receive a pat on the back or a few words of praise.

Vanity can also show itself in the tendency toward perfectionism. Often, those who are vain feel the need to see themselves reflected in the mirror of their own deeds. Perfectionism is different from mere attention to detail. It is obsessive. The amount of time and effort spent on a simple task goes beyond what is reasonable or necessary, all with the sole intent of looking good, even if only to oneself.

The last characteristic of vanity is an inclination to despise other people's vanity. In truth, no one is better at detecting a person's vanity than another vain person, and no one gets angrier when confronted with another person's vanity. What makes other people's vanity insufferable for other vain persons is that they see it as a zero-sum game. Any recognition given to others detracts from their own.

It is impossible to hide one's vanity for long. Sooner or later, the vain will find themselves cornered. Their words, behaviors, and attitudes end up betraying them, making evident their emptiness, delusion, and fantasy. Vanity is as insubstantial as smoke.

Am I vain?

- Do I have an obsessive need to look good in front of others?

- Am I overly concerned about the appearance of my body, clothes, or personal grooming? Do I invest more time and money in my appearance than I should?

- Do I brag about my intelligence, knowledge, or schooling in any area?

- Am I ostentatious? Do I show off clothing, jewels, or flashy possessions?

- Am I overly concerned about being ridiculed?

- Do I lose my nerve easily in front of others for fear of what they might think?

- Am I addicted to applause, to showing up in photos, or to any other sort of public recognition?

- Have I ever found myself begging for praise?

- Am I a perfectionist in things that are not really important?

12. SELF-RELIANCE

Doing It All Yourself

We all know people who have great composure and confidence. They radiate self-confidence. When self-confidence exceeds certain limits, however, it becomes distorted. It turns into self-reliance. This happens when we refuse to admit that we are dependent on other people. In fact, in the deepest recesses of the self-reliant person's psyche, there seems to be an incessant echo of a deep personal conviction: "I don't need anybody or anything."

Self-reliance is a form of pride. It's the expression of a heavy, sturdy, solid, and overgrown ego. The self-reliant are unaware of their limits, shortcomings, and needs. They consider themselves intelligent, strong, and well-prepared to pursue any enterprise all on their own. It is not unusual for self-reliant people to overestimate their capability.

Not long ago, I met a five-year-old boy who was a whiz kid. He was intellectually gifted, clever, and possessing a singular charm, but perhaps too aware of his potential. We were roaming around a ranch in a small jeep when the engine stopped running right before a steep slope. Even before the driver grabbed the cell phone to call for help, the child was opening the hood of the jeep to fix it. He had no experience with or knowledge of engines but was sure he could do it. His father had to raise his voice to keep him from sticking his small hands in the engine's boiling hoses.

The self-reliant person has built-in protection against criticism, a trait that distinguishes him or her from the prideful and the vain. Such a person has an ego that builds its own fortress and surrounds it with a deep and wide moat that isolates it within its own castle. While vain people worry about other people's opinions, self-reliant ones could not care less: "They can say whatever they please!"

The self-reliant person is resolute. Self-management is central. The slogan "do it yourself" defines how he or she approaches every task in life. A self-reliant person does not seek anybody's help because this individual considers no one apt or suitable to provide it, usually preferring to solve problems alone. Those who are self-reliant blindly believe in their own judgment and never asking for advice. If anyone tries to offer an opinion, they hit a brick wall. They would choose to drown rather than ask for help. Unable to acknowledge their precarious situation, they cannot accept a helping hand. In their minds, they label any help they might receive as pity and accepting it an unbearable humiliation.

Another common sign of self-reliance is recklessness. Self-reliant persons do not assess risk. They expose themselves to dangerous situations and assume tasks and challenges that are beyond them due to a pattern of overestimating their own abilities. At times, the self-reliant commit themselves to ventures so far out of their league that it becomes amusing, or even mortifying, to others. They, however, stay free and easy. The mighty and impetuous ego of a self-reliant individual throws itself like a kamikaze in the pursuit of his or her unattainable goal, choosing to die before admitting defeat.

Self-reliance is individualistic. It chooses working alone instead of teamwork as a result of seeing others not only as no help but also even as obstacles. Whenever possible, this kind of person takes on professional responsibilities that allow him or her an ample range of action and decision. A self-reliant person will pursue individual sports over team sports, and if coerced to join a team, will aim to play positions that allow for more individual achievement and glory.

Those who are self-reliant find it difficult to give themselves over to God. Notions of faith and trust in God seem too naïve to them. They believe that their life is and always must be under their own control. They forget that the essence of religion is acknowledging, accepting, and increasing reliance on God. In such immaturity, the self-reliant person believes that salvation is in his or her own hands. Popular phrases such as "God helps those who help themselves" make more sense to a self-reliant individual than Scripture-based ones like, "Ask and it will be given to you" (Matthew 7:7) and, "Without me you can do nothing" (John 15:5).

A constant display of self-reliance is, in many cases, nothing but a defense mechanism to flee from vulnerability. To acknowledge dependence on others is to expose oneself to being let down and to disappointment. By running away from such threats, the self-reliant anticipate and impose on themselves the punishment they most fear: isolation and abandonment.

It is not possible to hide neediness for long. Sooner or later, as a result of life's difficulties, the self-reliant person's fortress cracks and ends up crumbling, exposing frailties and vulnerability. At this point, some acknowledge their situation and accept help. Others run away in desperation.

Perhaps it's a matter of point of view. The self-reliant person is not aware that in reality reciprocal interdependence generates love, closeness, and ties with others. It is the catalyst for the most fruitful and intimate personal relationships, and is the cement that holds social bonds together. Furthermore, Jesus asserted that, "Amen, I say to you, unless you turn and become like children, you will not enter the kingdom of heaven" (Matthew 18:3). There is no one more dependent on others than a child.

Am I self-reliant?

- Do I feel too sure of myself, my talents, and abilities?

- Do I choose to suffer over asking for help?

- Do I frequently undertake tasks or challenges beyond my capacity?

- Am I an individualist? Do I avoid teamwork because I think others are more an obstacle than a help?

- Do I frequently encase myself in my own ideas and views about life?

- Do I care too little about what others think of me?

- Do I ever ask for advice?

13. HYPERSENSITIVITY

A Swollen Ego

At times, we all can be very touchy. "I got up on the wrong side of the bed," we say. We're not in a good mood. This is normal. Our moods can vary with a change in weather, worries, hormones, and even digestion.

Hypersensitivity is different. It relates to a swollen ego. Any organ becomes hypersensitive when swollen. The same thing happens to the ego. When it becomes swollen, the slightest thing hurts it. Hypersensitivity is more than just a bruised ego. It is an outlook and an attitude on life. Hypersensitive persons are under the impression, and even have the conviction, that people, events, and circumstances have conspired, like an invisible hand, to steal their peace and make their lives miserable.

Hypersensitivity affects all aspects of an individual's life. Its foundation is the imagination. The hypersensitive read into everything. Such a person ponders, speculates, presumes, and connects the dots too easily, reaching definitive conclusions based on just a few hints, often outside of the realm of reality. In addition, that imagination does not act alone. It goes hand in hand with a "victim complex" or delusions of persecution. This perspective makes a hypersensitive person perceive everything as aggressive, offensive, humiliating, or inconsiderate. In other words, everyone is out to hurt him or her.

The hypersensitive person's paranoid imagination causes feelings of being watched, criticized, and gossiped about. Hypersensitive individuals feel as if they are always the subject of gossip, the topic of everybody's conversations, but not as an object of praise.

Another common sign of hypersensitivity is the temper tantrum, a fleeting but explosive rage, vented at full volume and with dramatic bodily gestures. People who may appear otherwise calm, mature, and self-contained can protest violently and make disproportionate or even infantile gestures at the slightest hint of criticism.

I was colleagues with a very skilled and competent professor of medicine. I had only ever seen him behave professionally and in a rational manner, until one day I came to visit him. He had just been informed that the case he proposed for the weekly clinical seminar had not been chosen. I walked in on him having a colossal blowout. He ranted, punching the wall and stomping his feet. It was embarrassing, even comical, to see a man of his reputation acting like a small child. Undoubtedly, the central figure of this tragic comedy was his wounded ego.

The hypersensitive person tends to blow problems out of proportion. Ordinary predicaments become epic dramas. This individual blames life, other people, and him- or herself. Because of this perspective on life, resentment takes root in the heart. The hypersensitive person normally holds on to a keen recollection of past suffering, remembering every offense. Finally, when collecting on debts, the hypersensitive mixes them all together, recent transgressions with old ones, large and small, real and imagined. The hypersensitive person revels in chewing on the bitter herbs of the past. I believe that deep in this psychology lies a hidden masochism that gives such a person a certain amount of pleasure in rubbing perceived wounds. When feeling hurt, he or she enjoys embellishing this suffering with stories of imaginary betrayal.

Living in harmony with a hypersensitive person is a challenge. Marriage can become the antechamber to hell. Perhaps a husband does not even suspect what is going through his wife's mind until there is a blowup. A mere trifle is enough to declare war and pull out the big guns. Every fight is followed by a flood of suspicions, apprehensions, and accusations that have been kept secret until now, when these are finally let loose on a stunned and speechless husband. After a few bouts of venting, though, the situation can become complicated and oversensitivity takes hold of the relationship. Communication deteriorates and becomes habitually tense.

A while back, I counseled an older man who would say to me in frustration, "No matter what I do or say, my wife will use it against me." Because every word, behavior, or attitude can be interpreted, processed, and distorted in the overactive mind of a hypersensitive spouse, there is no room to say or do anything, because there is no knowing what might offend or hurt the spouse's feelings. The hypersensitive person irrationally believes he or she possesses a strange ability to penetrate and sense the core of the other's intentions without a chance of error.

Hypersensitivity eats away at the heart. It is this effect of hypersensitivity that explains the wear and tear in the relationships of some couples. The heart becomes weary and empty when hypersensitivity gives way to suspicion, suspicion to accusation, accusation to argument, and eventually argument to hatred.

Am I hypersensitive?

- Do I tend to misconstrue other people's behavior? Normally against me?

- Do I easily become resentful when I feel disregarded?

- Do I need to be treated with kid gloves to avoid being hurt?

- Do I take everything personally? Do I live with a defensive attitude because of it?

- Do I tend to magnify the small problems or difficulties in life?

- Do I throw temper tantrums when people do not treat me as I feel they should?

- Do I believe people are out to get me?

- Do I often complain of my bad luck?

- Am I resentful?

- Do I find a certain amount of pleasure in reopening my wounds?

14. REBELLIOUSNESS

The Desire to Be Contrary

The rebel is a person whose pride is unsatisfied. Proud people, as we have seen, place themselves above everyone else. The rebel, however, is often motivated by a different desire. Rather than stand out above all others, the rebel prefers to stand away from the crowd. Consequently, this person finds the mask of eccentricity as the easiest way to achieve his or her goal, despite the possibility of costly consequences.

The rebel is by definition opposed to what is considered normal or conventional, to being like everyone else. The customary approach is to oppose, or at the very least, distinguish him- or herself from other people. Rebels think they are famous every time someone calls them original. Rebels are not bothered at all by people saying they are different. What bothers them is if they don't say it loud enough.

There are, without a doubt, situations in which rebelliousness is honorable and justified. When the general attitude of a society is a thoughtless herd mentality and people are subjected to social manipulation, rebelliousness can be an ethical imperative and swimming upstream heroic. Nelson Mandela, Mahatma Gandhi, and Martin Luther King were all great rebels of their day. Their rebelliousness was a mature and well-justified one. It was not motivated by selfish aspirations. Rather than standing out from the crowd on their own, they wanted to get others to stand with them in a new way of thinking. They stood for and defended their causes even when it cost them great suffering and humiliation. But because their rebelliousness was righteous and sincere, their efforts bore fruit. The rebelliousness that we refer to in this chapter is a different breed. It relates to an immature rebelliousness, or as these people are sometimes called, "rebel without a cause." This type of rebel is mediocre and drab. He or she wants to be somebody, climbing into the limelight and getting people's attention by assuming affected postures, unusual attitudes, and contrived looks.

There are exotic rebels. They go out dressed outlandishly, with multicolored hair and tattooed skin. Parallel to their looks are their motivations. They feel proud to tout lost causes, the more futile the better. If such causes were to be successful or mainstream, these would cease to be uniquely rebellious.

It is not uncommon for this type of rebelliousness to become widespread. In fact, in recent decades, we have as a society witnessed the emergence of many groups, especially among young people—hippies, punks, goths, emos, and many others—who search for originality and individual identity. Although sometimes motivated for righteous reasons, there is always an element in these groups that is seeking nothing more than to be a garish splash on the tapestry of society. They segregate themselves not as a result of being marginalized by society but because it is part of their style. Their clothing, hairstyles, gestures, style, and language are like their fingerprints.

I worked for a while as a paramedic for the Red Cross in Tijuana, Mexico. I remember helping a gang member who had been hurt in a street fight. When I asked him for his address, he said to me, "I hang down on the Revu, but my hood is La Obrera." What he meant was, "I spend my time on Revolution Avenue, but live in the Obrera neighborhood." Even hurt, this gang member held fast to the culture of his rebelliousness.

A more common type of rebel is the homemade one. This rebel is not quite as extravagant but much more skilled in the use of subtle ploys to stand out. Thus, in a discussion in which the prevailing opinion is "A," the rebellious person will systematically choose "B" as a point of view whether he or she agrees with it or not. The rebel's posture is very particular, always taking a dissenting view. This habit soon becomes unconscious, and whenever the rebel does not actually contradict, this person will end up making some sort of distinction or correction to what has been said. When everyone else in the room says a wall is red, the rebel clarifies and insists it is only "reddish."

In a rebel's personal wardrobe, culinary tastes, travels, and entertainment, there is no room for anything traditional or common. There must be some exotic or distinctive detail to set the rebel apart. Intellectually, the rebel tends to identify with antiestablishment literature, countercultural ideologies, and radical choices. Professionally, innovation without collaboration is the thing. A rebel's ultimate dream is to introduce new paradigms and to recreate everything. In the religious realm, he or she flees from what is traditional in search of eccentric novelties or alternative spiritual currents.

Another typical trait of the rebel is mania. Mania is an obsessive and impulsive fixation for doing things, however simple, in a very peculiar way. It is not uncommon for the rebel to change the most habitual tasks into odd and even solemn rituals. The more this occurs, the more the rebel becomes difficult to deal with, maladjusted, and rigid. Everything must conform to the rebel's affected ways and habits. Living with him or her becomes complicated.

Rebelliousness is, paradoxically, a prevailing form of inauthenticity. Rebels perceive themselves as authentic, when in reality they are going along with the crowd. Where the majority goes, rebels will too, but in the opposite direction. In this way, rebels end up being more servile to trends than any conformist. They are totally conditioned by other people. When I was a child, two teenagers very prone to this behavior lived across the street. My siblings and I were entertained by their weirdness. It was during the 1970s when, for a while, platform shoes were the rage, even for men. Driven by our supposed admiration, these teenagers sported brand new and even higher platforms every week. They would show up with a measuring stick on hand to shock us with their four-inch soles. Nobody owned shoes as tall as theirs. Sadly, eccentricity has little to do with real human stature.

Am I a rebel?

- Do I regularly have the need to set myself apart from others?

- Do I like to be called original?

- Do I have somewhat eccentric tastes in the way I dress, speak, or eat?

- Do I go out of my way to oppose the majority opinion?

- Have I ever been a "rebel without a cause?"

- Am I selectively attracted to everything considered alternative (for example, alternative medicine, new-age spirituality, alternative diets, avant-garde fashion)?

- Do I easily align myself with antiestablishment groups, counter-cultural movements, or radical political factions?

- Do I adopt vocabulary or actions specifically to seem original?

- Do I tend to turn otherwise common tasks into rituals or extravagant personal practices?

ACCEPT
YOURSELF

15. ACCEPTANCE

True Self-esteem

Disappointments are part of life. There are times when people or circumstances do not measure up to our expectations. Perhaps we hoped for something different, something better, such as an ideal husband or wife, well-behaved children, an unconditional friend, a loyal business partner, or an honest service provider. However, life is full of surprises and letdowns. Our disappointment is more painful the closer and more beloved the person is who fails us.

There are also plenty of times when we disappoint ourselves. At any given moment, we are attacked by the idea that we are not what we are supposed to be, nor what we hoped to be, not to mention what we professed or believed ourselves to be. Hope fades with disappointment. The heart falls into heavy darkness and slips toward an existential crisis.

We dealt with the principal vices that emerge from the human heart in the first part of this book. It is now time to take a courageous first step. The preceding list attempted to reflect our reality in a precise manner. It is now time to act with sincerity to acknowledge it. That is the goal of this second part, a mature act of personal acceptance. It will be a brief reflection, necessary before delving into the third and much more positive part of this book.

To really accept ourselves, we must face the truth without glossing over or retouching our faults and failings. This demands honesty, humility, and courage. The process may be difficult and painful. Many choose denial over having to admit they are flawed.

I recall a fairly young woman who came seeking spiritual guidance from me. She was experiencing a difficult period in her marriage. As a preliminary step, I tried to help her evaluate her personal situation before examining her marital situation. We were not able to go far. As soon as we came close to unmasking her own inner faults, she abandoned the process. She did not show up for her next appointment, unable or unwilling to accept what she saw.

We must accept ourselves, even when it is difficult, if only for the sake of our mental health. Otherwise, we will be walking around in a state of delusion. By choosing to deny our flaws, we are setting ourselves up for personal, marital, or family tragedy, perhaps sooner than later.

Personal acceptance is a sign of maturity. Life, with its challenges and circumstances, reveals our strengths and capabilities, as well as our limits. It is a continuous lesson in humility that makes us more objective and realistic. Realism and objectivity are reliable indicators of our degree of maturity.

Thankfully, not everything in this process is painful. The path to self-discovery is also filled with positive surprises. Unknown aptitudes, potential, and talents come to light. These resources have been there, hidden and dormant, awaiting the opportunity to surface.

Self-acceptance is also an act of justice toward God, who made each one of us suitable to our vocation and mission in life. He does not make mistakes in his creations. He gave each one of us all that is necessary to realize ourselves fully. He did not give us our vices or obstacles, but he can help us turn these into positive traits, even if it takes us a long time to see those positive traits revealed. In the same way, just because God did not give us a particular skill, talent, or appearance does not mean we have been denied, but that God has something else in store for us. We could call this "the gift of not being."

I have a personal confession to make about this concept. I used to fall in love very easily during my adolescence and young adulthood. My friends knew it and even made fun of me for it. Now, among my group of friends there were two who stood out for their good looks. Girls would go crazy over them, but these young men did not pay much attention to their admirers. By contrast, another friend and I, who would have jumped at the chance, did not have that kind of charisma. Due in part to my passion for emergency medicine and in part because none of the girls I was interested in were interested in me, I dedicated most of my young adulthood to volunteering as an emergency medical technician for the Red Cross. This was the first step in a chain of events that ultimately led to my current priestly vocation. I ask myself sometimes what would have become of me if I had had more charm with girls. Perhaps the gift of not being in that immature time of my life kept me from taking the wrong path.

Acceptance does not mean, as some believe, having low self-esteem. Besides being an injustice to God, as mentioned earlier, low self-esteem can keep us from using our gifts to become the person God created us to be. Not appreciating the specific gifts that God has given us can also lead us to work day and night to be like other people who have different gifts than we do. We can end up being a stressed-out, imperfect, and unsatisfied imitation of a person we were never meant to be in the first place. As dangerous and as mistaken as low self-esteem can be, high self-esteem, the opposite extreme, can prove to be more dangerous. The history of more than a few "great men" teaches us clearly enough about the terrible long-term consequences of megalomania.

Accepting oneself means having neither high nor low, but realistic self-esteem. One must avoid extremes. Balance is not an easy task, especially when we give so much importance to what others may think or say about us. Centuries ago, in his book *The Imitation of Christ*, Thomas à Kempis wrote a phrase that is surprisingly relevant today and could do a lot of good if printed on billboards everywhere: "Praise adds nothing to [who you are], nor does blame take anything from it. You are what you are, and you cannot be said to be better than you are in God's sight."

True self-esteem consists of recognizing, valuing, and appreciating who we are with objectivity and gratitude, nothing more or less. It is here where self-esteem merges with humility, because humility is truth. We struggle at times, wasting precious energy, attempting to model a false image of ourselves. We give ourselves too much importance in an effort to prove to ourselves that we are what we really are not.

Self-acceptance is the price of freedom and the source of inner peace. Only those who accept and loves themselves for who they are can enjoy true freedom. As accurately stated by G.K. Chesterton: "Angels fly because they take themselves lightly.

Seven Habits for Acceptance

1. Learn to face your reality without touchups: Take a reality check!

2. Do your best to discover your aptitudes, potential, and talents, and try to develop them.

3. Seek to be realistic and objective about your limits and inabilities.

4. Cultivate profound gratitude for all the gifts you have received from God, without forgetting the gift of not being what you are not.

5. Concern yourself less about what other people say or might say about you.

6. Learn not to take yourself too seriously.

7. Learn to laugh at yourself now and then.

16. The Dominant Flaw

Unmasking the Enemy

Deep inside, we knew it all along. Contemplating the genealogic tree of vices, we realize that we have a bit of everything. We all have our moments when we are somewhat lazy, intemperate, sensual, comfort seeking, greedy, arrogant, vain, self-sufficient, hypersensitive, and rebellious.

We all do have a prevailing flaw or vice that rules our lives. It is what we call the "dominant flaw." It does not point to the ugliest or most serious deed we have committed in life. Certain sins may be very horrifying, but if only sporadic, these sins do not constitute a vice. The dominant flaw is a true vice, a persistent bad habit that shows its face every day.

Our dominant flaw, for obvious reasons, has a lot to do with our temperament. Passionate temperaments tend to fall more easily into pride and sensuality. Phlegmatic ones, on the contrary, are inclined toward laziness and an excessive fondness for comfort.

The discovery and acceptance of our own dominant flaw is a matter of maturity and honesty. Additionally, it is also a matter of strategy. Nobody has the focus or energy to fight on several fronts simultaneously. Flaws must be broken down and isolated to be combated effectively, following the slogan of the Roman legions, "divide and conquer." As the common spiritual adage goes: "If every year we would root out one vice, we would soon become perfect."

One vice a year! It seems easy. But realistically, getting control over, not to mention eradicating, our dominant flaw can be a lifelong pursuit. Our dominant flaw often dies with us. Briefly reviewing the development of our personality will help us to better understand why.

According to scholars of evolutionary psychology, a five-year-old child already carries 75 percent of the fundamental basis of his or her personality, including genetic and congenital elements as well as the environmental factors assimilated during early childhood. Nonetheless, at that age it is impossible to predict the child's personality, much less a dominant flaw. The decisive factors, although present, lie dormant.

When a child becomes an adolescent, it seems all the vices spring up at once. It is for this reason that the word "adolescence" reminds us of suffering. The adolescent can be simultaneously lazy, lustful, comfort seeking, vain, hypersensitive, and to top it off, rebellious.

The turbulence of this stage paves the way to emerging adulthood from ages sixteen to twenty years. The psychophysical development begins to culminate. Our personality becomes established as well as character traits, including whether we are calm or hot-tempered, or emotional or impassive, our disposition, tendencies, and inclinations, together with our dominant flaw.

The second phase of emerging adulthood, from ages twenty to thirty years, brings about continued melding of these elements. According to many authors on the subject, our personality crystalizes at the age of thirty. Beyond any debate, we can be sure that by age forty we are who we are and as the popular saying goes: "A tiger can't change its stripes."

Do we have no option but to remain as we are? Actually, there is a lot we can do. The dominant flaw is a challenge that offers us the very best opportunity to practice virtue every day, specifically that virtue we need most. The dominant flaw and the opposing virtue will become the axis on which we devise a life plan.

Now this brings us to the following question: How do we uncover our dominant flaw? Some people can identify it relatively easily. They are highly introspective. They observe themselves objectively and are able to discern their inclinations, tendencies, appetites, and moods. They know how to evaluate themselves. Those who have this capacity have solved a good part of the problem already.

There are others who require outside help. They need someone close who, in an atmosphere of trust and kindness, helps them discern their dominant flaw. This other person may be their spouse—who knows them so well!—or a good friend, or better yet, a spiritual director. This support is a source of light and objectivity, as no one is a sound judge of their own cause.

It is also possible to fine tune your introspective ability. All you need is a method, a technique of personal monitoring for a reasonable amount of time of two to four weeks. It consists of taking notes on all negative reactions or attitudes throughout a day. A negative reaction or attitude is anything that feels like anger, frustration, sadness, aggravation, despair, or unrest. Afterward, label it. Negative reactions are almost always rooted in one of the previously described vices or flaws. For example, impatience may be a sign of arrogance. Sensuality or lust may provoke uneasiness, agitation, or angst. Laziness may bring about a sense of unwillingness, apathy, or annoyance. A feeling of being wounded is typical of being hypersensitive.

It's useful to write down the results on a sheet of paper and keep track day by day. Before bedtime, write down the flaw or flaws that stood out during the day. At the end of a week or month, you will be able to corroborate which flaw has been the most recurrent. It is highly probable this will turn out to be your dominant flaw.

MODEL FOR A TABLE TO DISCOVER YOUR DOMINANT FLAW

Flaw	1	2	3	4	5	6	7
Laziness		X		X	X		X
Intemperance	X						
Lust				X			
Comfort seeking	X	X			X		
Greed							X
Arrogance		X					
Vanity					X		
Self-reliance	X						
Hypersensitivity						X	
Rebelliousness							

The numbers correspond to the days of the month or week. In this example, as you can see, the most recurring flaw is laziness.

IMPROVE YOURSELF

17. VIRTUES

Crucial Victories

Virtues are victories. They are the spoils of that long and hard-fought battle called life. "There is no greater virtue nor no nobler victory than to master and subdue one's own nature," as the French historian and soldier Pierre de Bourdeille, seigneur de Brantôme, once wrote. When reason prevails over impulse, excellence over mediocrity, and constancy over fickleness, then there is virtue.

A virtue is a good moral habit. Virtues are forged and strengthened through repetitive action. They crystallize into a stable behavior, a personal style. According to philosophers, virtue is a second nature, a way of being that wells up spontaneously or naturally. A well-rooted virtue is an anchor against the fluctuation of our instincts and the destructive forces of our intense passions.

Virtues do not flourish from one day to another. They require weeks, months, or even years to develop. Some virtues are perhaps more attainable because they agree with our personality. However, they normally require effort, discipline, sacrifice, and stubborn perseverance. Sir Edmund Hillary was the first person to conquer the peak of Mount Everest, but he didn't do that by just passing through on his way to somewhere else. These accomplishments are dreamed of, planned, prepared, and executed with clear and firm determination.

A virtue, even a modest one, is worth more than a heroic act, as great as it may be. In the right circumstances, it's possible that many of us would be capable of at least one heroic act big enough to get media attention. That is how everyday heroes are born. Virtue follows a very different process. Acts that forge a virtue are normally neither grand nor flashy, but quiet and disguised in the monotony of everyday life.

Once attained, a virtue is not ensured forever. A little carelessness can ruin it. This is part of the human drama. We are always in danger of relapsing, of slipping back down part of the slope we have already climbed.

Fortunately, behind these relapses—if you don't give in to them—there is a hidden principle that is key to personal growth, starting over. It's a fundamental principle, because not making mistakes is nearly impossible. The story of Sisyphus is not as unreal as it may seem. This character from Greek mythology is sentenced to push a heavy boulder up a mountain, just to have it roll down as soon as he reaches the peak, and then start over again. This is a very accurate description of our reality. The boulder falls again, but our muscles get stronger.

We have spoken about the first two elements of the triad "know yourself," "accept yourself," and "improve yourself." We walked through, as in a gallery, the most common vices. We then insisted on the need to accept ourselves with calmness and realism. Now, we must enter another gallery, this one beautiful and luminous, where the virtues reside.

Let's not forget that one of the objectives of this book is to help us discover and battle our dominant flaw with a life plan. Therefore, we will walk through the hallways of this new gallery with great personal interest, much like looking for urgently needed medicine at a pharmacy. For every vice there is an opposing virtue that, although it might not cure it, will at least control it. Generally, opposite to sensuality is temperance, whereas opposite to pride is humility. Within sensuality, laziness opposes industriousness; intemperance, self-restraint; lust, chastity; excessive attachment to comfort, austerity; and greed, generosity. Pride brings us arrogance opposed by gentleness, vanity by humility, self-reliance by openness, hypersensitivity by a detachment of self, and rebelliousness by authenticity.

Considering that the virtue we need most is the one that opposes our dominant flaw, we can presume it will be the most challenging. It may even seem so unattainable that it tempts us to feel discouraged and prematurely defeated. This would be the case if it all depended on our personal strength. However, we can count on an additional support of extraordinary power, God's grace. For this reason, virtue is on a higher plane, the victory of good over evil, of grace over sin, and of God over the snares of the devil. Fortunately, more than anyone else, God dreams of seeing us mature, realized, fulfilled, and happy.

CONTRAST BETWEEN VICES AND VIRTUES

VICE	VIRTUE
Sensuality	Temperance
Laziness	Industriousness
Intemperance	Self-restraint
Lust	Chastity
Attachment to Comfort	Austerity
Greed	Generosity
Pride	Humility
Arrogance	Gentleness
Vanity	Humbleness
Self-reliance	Openness
Hypersensitivity	Detachment of Self
Rebelliousness	Authenticity

18. INDUSTRIOUSNESS

A Full Life

Life yields its best fruit in the well-tended orchard of industriousness. It is a well-known fact that quiet and constant work is more productive in the long run than feverish but erratic activity. Attitude is worth more than aptitude, and perseverance goes further than natural talent. Goethe once said that industriousness is nine-tenths inventiveness.

Industriousness, the opposite of laziness, means to apply ourselves with determination, dedication, and effectiveness to the tasks or responsibilities we face each moment. More than a singular virtue, industriousness is a set of dispositions and attitudes toward life's great undertakings as well as everyday duties.

Those who are industrious do not waste. They organize, plan, execute, create, invent, and cultivate. Such individuals take advantage of every opportunity. Life flashes by, and they know it. Time is limited, opportunities pass by and do not return, stamina weakens, and resources become depleted. These conditions are all part of our human limitations, but far from discouraging industrious persons, they inspire them with determination, momentum, and tenacity in all their tasks.

Industriousness comprises a variety of distinctive traits such as efficiency, thoroughness, perseverance, diligence, and order. Efficiency is the capacity to carry out a task or job with the least amount of energy and time yielding maximum performance and profit. Considering that our scarcest resource is time, efficiency can also be defined as doing more in less time. It seems easy, but it entails substantial concentration, discipline, and a clear sense of what is essential.

> It is imperative to know the value of time. There is a story about a man who, nearing the end of his life, yearned to go out on the street corner and beg for minutes to use for yet another project. "Just fifteen more minutes!" he would plead, like the ones so many people waste when they kill time. The man knew the value of that time well. Those quarters of an hour, when strung together, would add up to many hours.

The efficient person self-imposes attention to the clock in a healthy and steady race against time, but without getting stressed out. In fact, the race can actually be enjoyable when we are engaged in the right projects.

Our emphasis then changes when we go from efficiency to thoroughness, from doing more to doing it better. Thoroughness means to have care and constant dedication to doing things with excellence. It is the art of work, to complete a task with detail and good taste. Details are like a personal signature, as these leave a mark of our personality. Details are the pedestals of great souls.

Perseverance is firmness and constancy in our resolutions and enterprises. Always finish what you start. Perseverance demands an unusual strength of soul. It requires foresight and dealing with fatigue, obstacles, and difficulties as a normal part of any undertaking, including life itself. Beethoven, who knew something of the subject, said that what distinguishes a man as being worthy of the name is his perseverance in adverse and difficult situations. He continued to compose musical masterpieces even after he was unable to hear or perform them himself. His perseverance was rewarded. Immediately on the conclusion of the debut performance of his last and most famous symphony, he heard no applause. He felt frustrated. It was only when he turned to face the public that he became aware that they were giving him a standing ovation.

Diligence consists of dealing with our own responsibilities and tasks promptly and swiftly. An industrious person does not postpone important tasks until the following day. This person follows the principle of "not putting off to tomorrow what you can do today." His or her alarm clock never goes off twice in the morning. Industrious people seem to travel through life on greased rails. They give the impression of doing things with ease. It is as hard for them as for anyone else, but they have made it a habit to get things done instead of complaining.

Order is another aspect of industriousness. It is the discipline of keeping everything in its place, from personal belongings to calendar priorities. In a chaotic and frenzied world, order is a matter of survival. Classical wisdom coined a phrase that proves to be more relevant today than ever: Serva ordinem et ordo servabit te ("preserve order and order will preserve you").

The fruits of industriousness are instantly noticeable. Perhaps the first fruit is to feel excited about the work itself. A task that may have seemed difficult or uncomfortable at the onset, once the initial resistance is conquered, becomes pleasant and even enjoyable. The skills acquired are an excellent reward. As for everything else, all obstacles conquered turn into experiences of success.

The satisfaction gets multiplied when we open our horizons and place any task, even trivial ones, in the wider context of its significance. This is exemplified by an anecdote about three bricklayers who were asked what they were doing. The three were doing the same job, but their attitude and enthusiasm about the work was very different. The first one said: "I lay bricks." The second one phrased it as: "I'm raising a wall." Finally, the third one exclaimed excitedly: "I'm building a cathedral!"

A Test of Industriousness

- Do I get out of bed at once? Am I always on time?

- Do I have a clearly defined calendar? Do I make an effort to achieve more in less time? Do I feel accomplished at day's end?

- Do I keep my personal belongings, room, and desk in order?

- Do I subscribe to the motto: "Always finish what you start"?

- Do I prefer the stairs to the elevator when going to a nearby floor?

- Am I detail-oriented in the execution of my duties and responsibilities?

- Do I look for meaning in everything I do?

19. TEMPERANCE

Secrets for Enjoying Life

"Moderation in all things," as the saying goes. Maintaining the right balance, measure, and limits are acts of wisdom. This is not only because sooner or later we have to pay for our actions but also because refining our sensibility helps us to enjoy life's small pleasures more!.

Temperance is defined as moderation or self-restraint when satisfying bodily appetites. Therefore, it is not a matter of stoically repressing them, but of controlling them, channeling them, and keeping them within limits. Our appetites in and of themselves are good, but these need to be supervised by our intelligence and controlled by our will.

A practical rule of thumb to set a proper limit on bodily appetites is contained in St. Ignatius of Loyola's wise precept: "as much as...." One must eat, drink, sleep, rest, and so forth, as much as necessary to meet one's real physical needs, in other words, as much as is healthy. Any symptom of excess or overload indicates crossing the line into intemperance.

Food is perhaps the most difficult area for temperance. One must watch three aspects: quantity, quality, and scheduling. With regard to quantity, it is essential to cover the energetic, metabolic, and structural needs of the body. This requires variety, not just consuming what we like. It is wise to apply in this matter the well-known 80/20 rule: As long as we eat 80% of nutritious food, what we need, the rest may be what we like. In addition, experts usually recommend light, more frequent meals as opposed to fewer but larger ones. Ultimately, it is not a bad idea to make it a habit of leaving the table a little bit hungry.

In terms of scheduling, eating breakfast, lunch, and dinner at set times is more than a good habit. It is an intelligent way to arrange the day and to give it structure. And there is nothing better for the stomach than to feed it at regular times.

Drinking alcoholic beverages is not inherently bad, as some people suppose. There are alcoholic beverages that, in moderation, have a healthy effect on certain variables of the body. Many people enjoy the pleasant effect of a daily glass of good red wine on cholesterol levels. The key is to learn how to drink, which consists of not only drinking within limits in general but also knowing your own limits. Every person has a tolerance level for alcohol that depends on his or her particular physical makeup, psychological vulnerability, and even genetic predisposition. It is imperative to know that limit and not exceed it, regardless of how much others may drink or may pressure you to do so.

Addiction to drugs must be addressed separately. The topic is more complex and requires special care that goes beyond the scope of this book. At any rate, I can definitely say that an attitude of temperance in every aspect of life is the best way to prevent this tragic vice.

Temperance is a way of life. More than depriving yourself of this or that pleasure or whim, it is an attitude of enjoying everything in moderation, in the right measure. As a result, moderation becomes pleasurable and one experiences a sense of unique freedom. Christ himself knew to value, appreciate, enjoy, and share the legitimate pleasures that were availed to him at the time. We need only remember it was he who brought joy to a wedding by turning water into wine, and of the best quality, unlike any other in history.

The discipline of bodily appetites, frequently difficult and austere, sharpens our senses. Depriving ourselves of unnecessary pleasures fine-tunes our senses to be more open to enjoyment. This is the legitimate and enjoyable reward of a temperate life. In the end, pleasure is not found in things but in ourselves. The intemperate person, however, saturated and desensitized, requires progressively greater stimuli to achieve the same sensations.

Last, temperance is related to solidarity and compassion. By depriving ourselves of certain pleasures, we become more sensitive to the needs and hardships of others.

A good friend once told me about an incident he experienced while on vacation with his wife and three children at a well-known resort. While entering a restaurant to dine, a homeless child of roughly six years of age walked in alongside his children. The waiter quickly approached them with a less than friendly attitude. My friend became aware of the problem when he looked behind him. Moved by what he saw, he stopped the waiter in his tracks by telling him, "He is with us!"

The waiter could not hide his anger. He knew that "brat" constantly found his way into the restaurant to beg for money. My friend demanded that the child sit with his family at the dinner table, encouraging him to order whatever he wanted. Halfway through the meal, his wife noticed the child would only eat half of what was on his plate. When asked if he was not hungry, the child responded, "My mother and brothers are outside, and I want to take them something to eat." Touched even more deeply, they called the grumpy waiter and asked for a few more orders to go.

Sensitivity such as this cannot be improvised. One needs to have felt a bit of hunger, cold, and neediness to connect with the hunger, cold, and hardship of others. Generosity is the mature fruit of deprivation.

A Test of Temperance

- Do I follow the rule of "as much as" when eating, drinking, or resting?

- When drinking alcohol, do I stop at an appropriate limit?

- Do I make it a habit to leave the table without feeling "stuffed?"

- Do I follow a fairly regular eating schedule?

- Have I learned to enjoy the small pleasures in life?

- Do I try to say no even when something is technically allowed, so I can say no to those things that are always bad?

- Do I share generously even if it requires a certain amount of self-deprivation?

20. CHASTITY

The Guardian of Love

Chastity is a valiant virtue. It demands courage and bulletproof integrity. To abstain from illicit sexual pleasures in a world that offers them just a few mouse clicks or dollar bills away is not easy. In a comedy film, several young men made a bet about the possibility of abstaining from sex for forty days. They had taken for granted that chastity would be unbearable and practically impossible when not attempted with the appropriate spirit. Lewd scenes, provocatively dressed girls, and incessant lustful suggestions spread like mold throughout the movie would put this virtue to the test at every turn.

Perceived merely as the restraint of sexual impulses, chastity may seem, to say the least, like a repressive virtue. The genuine essence of chastity is different. It stems from a very positive, noble, and realistic view of sexuality. This positive and realistic perspective is what both sustains and demands this virtue. Without chastity, our sexuality is fractured and becomes easy to throw to the flames of lust.

Chastity is not an unnatural repression or unattainable ideal. Chastity means living our sexuality in a special way that expresses love, not denies it. We are designed to love, as we discussed in the first chapter. For this reason, we are sexual, etymologically differentiated as man or woman. In fact, not only our bodies are differentiated but also our psychology and even our spirit, because all of our being was designed to love.

Sexuality allows us to give ourselves fully in an interpersonal relationship that is the most intimate union possible.

There are obviously various ways of pursuing chastity according to our particular state in life. Married people practice chastity by living their conjugal intimacy with faithfulness and generosity. Marital chastity does not mean, as some believe, that the spouses must abstain from sexual relations except for purposes of procreation. Contrary to Stoicism and other schools of thought such as Gnosticism, Christianity has upheld and upholds the great value of sexual life in marriage as a joyous way of expressing love between the spouses.

Single or celibate people are also called to live their sexuality in their own way. They are called to experience its other dimensions, although not through sexual intimacy, such as the way in which each gender communicates, helps, supports, and welcomes others; in other words, the way they love.

We know that, as an effect of original sin, our sexuality ended up inclined toward sin, an inclination called "concupiscence." Since then, chastity has been a grueling fight. It is the battle of virtue against the schemes of our carnal desires and lustful incitements that surround us. This fight is at times so fierce that many see it as a lost cause. Victory, however, is possible.

More than willpower, chastity requires intelligence and strategy. Lust is not fought head-on. Those who entertain a dialogue with temptation to see if their will is strong enough to resist it are already stepping on a minefield. The best strategy is to avoid it. Remembering, resisting, and replacing are a good summary of this strategy. This means remembering that we are weak, to prudently avoid unnecessary dangers; resisting the impact of temptation serenely, focusing our mind on other affairs; and replacing bad habits with positive thoughts and healthy interests.

A particularly constructive way to cultivate chastity lies in creating a temptation-free zone, as circumstances allow, especially in our own bedroom and workplace by removing anything that might tempt us or give us access to temptation. Parents should also offer their children a temptation-free zone at home. Unfortunately, there seems to be a lot of naïveté in this regard. A preacher perhaps did not exaggerate when admonishing parents against the dangers of unrestricted television, internet access, or cell phones in their children's bedrooms or other private spaces when he said, "It's like letting a rattle snake loose in their bedrooms. Sooner or later they'll be bitten."

Another basic way to cultivate chastity is by having a balanced and demanding schedule of activities. Idleness is the root of all vices, as we well know, but its favorite child is lust. Managing time wisely and curtailing makeshift activities will leave little room for temptations. Apart from ordinary daily activities, a good amount of weekly exercise is advisable as well as pastimes or hobbies to allow for healthy entertainment and rest. Outings to the country or mountains to contemplate nature and its exceptional beauty are another way of keeping the mind and heart away from the tar pit of our distorted passions.

These are natural means. There are also spiritual ones, such as prayer, sacraments, and our filial devotion to the Blessed Virgin. Jesus stated that one should be vigilant and prayerful to avoid falling into temptation: "Watch and pray that you may not undergo the test. The spirit is willing, but the flesh is weak" (Matthew 26:41). Vigilance is imperative whenever one is not protected by an impenetrable fortress, and that is certainly the case with chastity. Vigilance means foreseeing and anticipating situations, detecting dangers, and running away at once from near occasions of sin. At times, however, that is not enough. One must pray for the support of God's grace to conquer, and if we falter, we must promptly pick ourselves back up. We must seek God's forgiveness, knowing that he is always "merciful and gracious...slow to anger, abounding in mercy" (Psalm 103:8).

Last, it is helpful to cultivate a victorious mindset. As long as we don't consciously and deliberately accept temptation, we are still on our feet. The evil one, in order to weaken us, leads us to believe that we have fallen, when in truth we are fighting. A victorious mindset goes hand in hand with a mature and serene attitude. Nervousness in the face of temptation is not helpful. We must remain calm and remember that God will not allow us to be tempted beyond our strength (see 1 Corinthians 10:13).

Modesty is chastity's cousin. For many people, perhaps too used to rampant immorality, the virtue of modesty has a medieval ring to it. Our society is still immature despite being twenty-one centuries old. It continues to be impressed by the seductive force of the erotic. Otherwise, the sex industry would be bankrupt! Modesty is a natural sheath to protect the treasure of our own intimacy from ignoble looks or attitudes. But more than a way of dressing, modesty is a way of looking. It means resting our eyes respectfully on our own body and that of others. Despite someone else's lack of modesty, our eyes can always remain modest. Modesty is the soul's skin, because modesty's purpose is not only to protect the body but also the spirit.

A Test of Chastity

- Do I take a positive view of chastity?

- Am I selective with the websites, television shows, newspapers, and magazines I allow into my home and life?

- Do I serenely look away when I see or suspect a danger to my chastity?

- Do I treat people with respect and consideration? Do I avoid familiarity with those who can tempt me to fall?

- Have I made a habit of focusing my thoughts, memories, and fantasies on positive and fruitful ideas?

- Do I cultivate modesty and discreetness in the way I dress? In the way I look at others?

- Have I made a good plan for my weekly schedule that keeps me busy all the time? Do I maintain a healthy balance of exercise and relaxation?

- Have I learned to enjoy nature?

21. AUSTERITY

Reeducating the Soul Through the Body

Life does not treat us all equally. Some people arrive in this world with a silver spoon. Others, the great majority, are born into more precarious situations. Later, life itself seems to trace diverse paths and create arbitrary distinctions between rich and poor, fortunate and unfortunate, and winners and losers

At any rate, austerity is a worthwhile virtue for all. Beyond our good fortune or lack thereof, we must all pursue this virtue to be able to face the normal inconveniences and limitations we encounter in life with peace of mind and a positive attitude.

Austerity may be viewed as the rational and moderate use of material possessions. Although austerity has to do, by definition, with a disciplined and severe attitude, it is perhaps the best and the most intelligent way of enjoying life. That is why the first trait of austerity is joy. An austere person knows how to enjoy and appreciate what he or she has been given, whether a lot or a little. Here, austerity goes hand in hand with gratitude. Experience confirms common sense in this regard. The richest person is not the one who has the most, but who needs the least. Austerity is the art of learning how to enjoy more with less.

A group of young students from our seminary in Rome were taking a break at a small bay south of Naples. With nothing more than the ocean and a few watermelons, they had so much fun that the onlookers were perplexed. A man aboard a luxurious yacht dove in and swam toward them to ask their secret. It turned out that he did not know what to do with his seventeen-year-old son who was dying of boredom aboard the luxury cruiser.

Children are excellent pupils in this matter if they are given the opportunity. They have fun with anything. A rag ball or broom stick is enough to dream up an adventure. Therefore, to overwhelm them with toys is a serious mistake. It is to steal from them nature's greatest gift, which is their imagination. The same happens with teens. The more sophisticated their entertainment demands, the more prone to boredom they will become.

A second trait of austerity is the ability to endure and tolerate physical difficulties. The austere person does not shy away from cold or heat, rain or shine, or sacrifice or shortage. This person is a tough cookie, and struggles and difficulties are par for the course. The austere person is prepared for anything. Nothing surprises, let alone discourages this person. In fact, difficulty often makes him or her more motivated and enthusiastic.

I was moved by the account of the first African American master diver of the United States Navy, whose story was chronicled in the movie *Men of Honor*. He was a cook who became a national hero. As his story began, he was seasoned in the school of contempt, humiliation, trials, and of course, the inclemency of the sea. His feat cost him his leg, but for him the loss was well-justified. It was a matter of honor.

Austerity is a typical trait of brave and adventurous spirits, who refuse to limit themselves to what is comfortable. They go further, climb higher, and dive deeper even if there are great sacrifices along the way. That is the reason austere people enjoy the privileges nature holds for those willing to pay the price of discomfort and hardship. Winning a medal, setting a record, or contemplating a sunrise atop a mountain peak are just a few examples.

Another healthy effect of austerity is that it purifies and frees our sensitivity. "Abundance makes me poor," said the ancient Roman poet Ovid. Comfort tires us and ends up setting into motion a life full of boredom. Austerity, however, awakens and sharpens sensitivity. We have all experienced it. Being deprived of some comfort for a period of time prepares us to enjoy it with renewed intensity.

Another fruit of austerity is flexibility. An enemy of the superfluous, austerity lives abundantly with only the essentials. Even in the absence of what is necessary, the austere heart always finds a reason to be happy. This is why it's so adaptable. Austere persons do not complicate their own life or the lives of others and cultivate the good habit of not complaining. They acknowledge, as suggested by the great Spanish novelist Pio Baroja, that self-denial is worth more than bitterness, frequently celebrating and appreciating any help received and not complaining that it could have been greater or better. Austerity allows you to enjoy all the flavors of life. It lets you relish the sun and rain, accept abundance and scarcity, rest on a king-size bed or curl up on a rickety old cot, and enjoy a five-star hotel or settle just as well into a sleeping bag on the floor.

A few years ago, while a seminarian, a visit to my family coincided with a surprise visit from an uncle and his wife. My parents gave up their bedroom and moved into mine, which at that time was empty, to accommodate them. At my arrival, I tried to convince my parents to allow me to take the living room sofa instead of staying in my old room. They did not allow it. At almost seventy years of age each, they took the living room and forced me to take my old bedroom. The living room sofa was not the most comfortable to sleep on for people their age or of any age. Nevertheless, they paid the price of discomfort and did so lovingly to provide me with the best accommodations possible.

Last, austerity helps us to rediscover enduring sources of happiness. A few months back, a coffee entrepreneur commented on having suffered the worst drought in 30 years. His plantation, however, had yielded the best coffee ever. He explained that, "Plants, during a drought, remember their roots." Facing austerity, perhaps after some time of prosperity, allows us to rediscover the joy of simple pleasures, moderation, and inexpensive fun. Material limitations awaken the pleasures of the spirit, reminding us "that man does not live by bread alone." It can even be the beginning of a new stage of spiritual growth, because the soul is often reeducated by the body. The growth is even more profound when that body is being reeducated by a demanding but exceptional teacher, austerity.

A Test of Austerity

- Do I habitually appreciate and enjoy what I have?

- Do I avoid the superfluous in my bedroom, office, leisure time, and elsewhere in my life?

- Do I have a sensible but limited wardrobe?

- Do I teach my children the value of austerity by my example? Do I teach them to sacrifice their own comfort for the comfort of others when appropriate?

- Do I avoid complaining about the weather if it doesn't suit my needs?

- Do I deprive myself occasionally of certain comforts I'm accustomed to in order to rediscover the joy of having them again?

22. GENEROSITY

The Hands of the Heart

Generosity is both the privilege and charm of great souls. Generous people captivate, encourage, and inspire us, leaving indelible traces on our hearts.

> There was once a small child, too young to read, who spent his allowance buying the newspaper from another child that sold them on a corner close to his house. His father asked him, "Why don't you buy candy or chocolates instead?" His son responded, "I buy the paper so that boy has something to eat."

Generosity is detachment from material possessions for the benefit of others. There is always someone who knocks on the door of our heart begging for a little love. They will ask perhaps for a bit of bread, some support, a sign of approval, a smile or an embrace, a few minutes of our time, or maybe even forgiveness. Many times, our reaction depends on the moment or mood we are in. It should not be this way. A generous soul is always ready to give what it can and frequently a little more. A generous heart is never locked.

Generosity is not improvised. Acts of detachment from material things are preceded by detachment from oneself. Only a heart that is detached from itself and its possessions is open and ready to give of itself to others. We must not forget that God is the boundless source of all generosity. He is love, and love, as theology teaches us, always tends to spread. The essence of love is the gift of self. In this sense, the generous heart is a reflection of the face of God. It reveals the presence of God at its core. More than an overabundance of material goods, generosity presupposes an overabundance of love. It does not consist of giving away leftovers but of sharing even the best of what we have.

> I remember a woman who sold candy on the streets and once approached my car while I was in line waiting to get gas. As I was lowering my window to decline her offer, she saw my clerical garb. "Are you a priest?" she asked. "Yes, may I help you?" I answered. "Please take one," she said maternally, "I want you to have it." I had to accept, quite moved, a little bag of peanuts that I kept as a sign of her generosity. Since that day, I have continued to pray for her and her family.

There are people who do not believe in generosity. They believe the world will not be changed by charity but by more profound structural transformations. Perhaps they have a point. Profound changes in the economic and social struc-tures of society are necessary to reduce hunger and poverty worldwide. There are institutions in place to channel aid and ensure its proper use. It is exciting to witness the flourishing of initiatives and foundations, both of a religious and social nature, designed to alleviate the struggles of people who are most in need. Supporting and volunteering for these institu-tions is an efficient way to live the virtue of generosity. None-theless, we must not forget the value of personal, face-to-face help whenever possible. This gives a human face to our generosity. A piece of bread given with a look of love can nourish much more than a hundred pieces given coldly. Authentic generosity transcends the material realm. It seeks to relieve all the needs and sufferings with which it comes into contact. There are those who need understanding and beg for approval. Others yearn to fix their broken reputation and beg for kind words. Others are in need of forgiveness and clamor for our hearts to forget a little. Of all these, forgiveness is the greatest gift we can offer. Forgiveness requires an unparalleled generosity, because it must be given freely and completely. We cannot give it with strings attached or bring up our grievance during a future argument. Once we forgive generously, we must also let go.

Internal joy is perhaps the most immediate fruit of generosity. On a certain occasion, a man confessed, "I sometimes feel selfish in my generosity. It is the only way I can be happy." Generosity is its own reward. It does not need compensation. The thing about generosity is, even though we act without expecting something in return, it has a boomerang effect. It always comes back to us. The more gratitude we show, the more love will be returned to us.

Some time ago, I met a man at church who looked homeless. Even though it was cold, he was only wearing a worn-out shirt, threadbare pants, and sandals. As I was leaving the church he approached me, but instead of asking for money he invited me to have breakfast at a nice restaurant. I thought he was joking or perhaps a little crazy. I respectfully refused, although he insisted he would be waiting for me there. Half an hour later, after having had breakfast on my own, I showed up at the restaurant, mostly out of curiosity. He was indeed there, sitting at a table covered with food and in the company of a well-dressed, beautiful woman. She was his wife. He invited me to sit and proceeded to tell me his story. He was really a successful businessman, the owner of two canned goods factories. He dressed as a homeless person until breakfast and suffered in the elements to remind himself of his humble beginnings and to keep his heart detached from the things material success can provide. Moments later, he asked his wife to write me a generous check to support priestly formation.

"Don't judge a book by its cover," as the saying goes. The same applies to generosity. It hides where we least expect it, but when it emerges it shows a person's true colors.

A Test of Generosity

- Do I see with my heart? Am I sensitive to other people's needs?

- Am I ready to be generous daily?

- Have I resolved to do a concrete act of generosity at least once a day?

- Do I donate to support a charitable institution (secular or religious)?

- Do I dedicate at least two of the 168 hours in a week to volunteering or evangelization?

- If I cannot help someone materially, do I at least offer kindness and courtesy? Do I make a point of giving warmth and love to everyone I meet?

- Am I convinced that I can always offer help regardless of circumstances?

23. MEEKNESS OF HEART

A Virtue of the Wise

Jesus Christ exemplified all human virtues during his time on earth. He embodied each one of them to the highest degree and without flaw. However, in his teachings he called explicit attention to this particular virtue: "Take my yoke upon you and learn from me, for I am meek and humble of heart; and you will find rest for your selves" (Matthew 11:29).

Meekness of heart is the opposite of selfishness. The latter, as we have observed, brings tension, imbalance, and dissent into all human relationships: with God, others, ourselves, and the world around us. More specifically, meekness contrasts arrogance, the attitude of superiority and intolerance toward others.°Δ1

Meekness of heart is perhaps the most visible expression of humility. It is a relaxed, peaceful, and serene attitude that springs from accepting ourselves and others just as we are. People who are meek of heart are filled with great internal tranquility. They make their way through life amid complete tranquility of order, which for St. Augustine was the definition of peace.

Meekness of heart is not the fruit of a passive attitude, quiet submission, or peace as the result of compromise. It is the fruit of a strong and courageous heart. You cannot achieve peace until you have conquered selfishness and its many ramifications, especially that twisted branch called pride, from which impatience, anger, irritability, and other explosions of temper emerge.

Meekness of heart has many characteristics, one being kindness. Such kindness is often confused and seen in a negative light as meekness or weakness, but this type of kindness or meekness is worth more than a heroic attitude. It contains iron-like qualities hidden under the appearance of natural goodness. Pope St. John XXIII, better known as the "good pope" due to his benevolence, is said to have revealed this secret to his confessor: "I consider kindness not merely a quality of the heart, but the reward of the work you do in here," he said touching his heart.

Graciousness is a nuance of kindness. It has to do with an amiable, pleasant manner expressed through showing a peaceful, calm face to others, a sincere smile, or a courteous gesture. For many, these are signs of good manners, yet deep down, these reflect a humble, meek, respectful, and considerate attitude toward others.

Yet another trait of meekness is empathy. Empathy means identifying yourself with the suffering of others, or as it is commonly said, putting yourself in someone else's shoes. An empathetic person is understanding, patient, and compassionate. This person perceives what others may be suffering or what burdens they might be carrying inside, and pays close attention so as not to hurt them. Moreover, when an empathetic person must correct another individual, he or she knows how to choose the most appropriate time, manner, words, and gestures.

The signature behavior of those who are meek is being of service in every way possible. If they possess natural leadership skills, they will use them to help, guide, support, and motivate. Theirs is not the leadership style of someone who tries to be everyone's buddy, always seeking to be appreciated and praised. On the contrary, it is a demanding style, yet very respectful in dealing with others and with an optimistic appreciation of their colleagues. They try to apply the wise Latin adage: *Suaviter in modo, fortiter in re* ("gently in manner, strongly in deed").

Another aspect of meekness of heart is patience. This virtue may be defined as the ability to work with other people's mistakes and limitations without getting upset. Patience is reflected above all in the way we look at someone whose indiscretion, lateness, neediness, slowness, or any other personal flaw may inconvenience or irritate us. The meek of heart, of course, react gently. They do not become flustered or irritated and do not allow themselves to be swayed by anger.

Gentleness of heart may be the missing link in the process of forgiveness. People who are meek of heart forgive extraordinarily easily. This is because by being meek they have the basic resource for forgiveness, which is acceptance. Given that some resentments can be justified and some perceived hurts valid, we must be able to accept them before we can truly forgive. Meekness in itself does not heal wounds, but it nurtures the healing power of acceptance. It means ceasing to fight with reality—with the incidents and wounds that can't be changed—and instead acknowledging and absorbing them.

Meekness carries with it a liberating principle of life: "No one owes me anything." Because generous people are detached from their own needs and wants, such people are able to place others at the center of their lives. On this account, it is possible to understand the reason why the meek of heart can feel that everything is OK.

A Test of Meekness

- Do I usually look with kindness on others?

- Am I particularly careful with my choice of words and gestures to reflect kindness?

- Do I keep an inner calm when having to correct someone?

- Do I keep my composure when dealing with someone else's mistakes?

- Do I try to forgive immediately when someone hurts or offends me?

- If in a position of authority, do I attempt to be meek in manner and strong in deed?

- Do I make it a habit to forgive with mercy?

24. Humility

Intelligent Simplicity

Humility is a precious gem. It has a captivating power. Humble people are well-liked by everyone. In the same way the vain antagonize and isolate, the authentically humble person attracts, captivates, and draws in others.

The virtue of humility is not easy to define. The concept, however, evokes naturalness, candor, and authenticity. It is exactly the opposite of complexity, phoniness, and affectation. Humility inspires relaxed and spontaneous personalities, without fears or complexes.

Humility contrasts with arrogance and presumption. Humble people cultivate their talents and qualities, including outstanding ones, with ease. Everything they do, even if it is extraordinary, is done with an attitude of modesty and ordinariness. Pretentious people tend to go in the opposite direction. They like to create the appearance that everything they do is extraordinary, even if it's nothing out of the ordinary.

Many truly great individuals have been, first and foremost, humble people. They have been able to magically appear unassuming. I remember how Pope John Paul I, the "smiling pope," captivated worldwide attention with his humble personal demeanor. His papacy only lasted 33 days—one of the shortest in history—but his humility left a profound imprint on the entire world.

Humble people take pleasure in transparency. They present themselves as they are, without pretensions. They do not wear masks or disguises to distort reality. They do not try to be what they are not. They always stay in the realm of truth and genuine acknowledgement of who they are. Their attitude does not come from resignation but from relishing their reality. Therefore, humble people tend to resist any feelings of inferiority. In fact, they are uncomplicated people who recognize the value, competence, and even superiority of others without feeling any less valuable themselves. They enjoy praising, pondering, and highlighting the positive qualities of others. Praising others is second nature for them.

Accordingly, humble people normally have a strong sense of their own personal dignity. In their humility, they feel self-assured, confident, and satisfied with themselves. They do not put themselves forward or resort to flattery to earn a few pats on the back or cheap applause.

Another typical trait of the humble person is the ability to acknowledge mistakes without evasion or cover-up. The humble rarely try to justify themselves and are mature enough to know that "to err is human" and that often in life more is learned from mistakes than from getting things right. Apart from that, frequently it is the case that silencing an initial mistake leads to other more serious ones. Humility breaks the first link of that chain of mistakes.

Trust is another privilege of humble people. It is what we could also call "intelligent naiveté." Humble people prefer to err by thinking the best of someone than by attributing bad intentions to their motives. They favor living in an atmosphere of trust instead of one of fear, worry, and suspicion, which always carries a degree of irrationality.

Humble people do not fear looking bad, which is perhaps the reason they seldom do. When they need to expose themselves to mockery or ridicule, they do so. Fear of humiliation does not inhibit or paralyze them. They know that a certain dose of ridicule can help you let go of fear and act with complete freedom, free from the fear of what people may say.

Humble people enjoy great internal peace. They know and accept themselves and make a sincere effort to improve themselves. This mindset promotes serenity. They do not cook up unrealistic aspirations or impossible dreams. They are realistic about their possibilities and limits, and so they rarely experience frustration. They react to adversity without drama or wild theatrics. They weigh situations, place them in proper context, and act accordingly. They handle setbacks naturally and decisively, knowing that these are part of life.

Humble people who are naturally shy or inhibited take advantage of every opportunity to overcome their timidity. Perhaps a gathering of friends could be an opportunity to tell a story, make a comment, or tell a joke. If at first they feel insecure or stiff, they are certain that time will reward them with more confidence and assuredness.

Humble people flee from complexity. Simplicity, on the contrary, is characteristic of angels. God is absolute simplicity. Perhaps we should attempt to find the common denominators of our worries and simplify them as much as possible. A simpler look at our lives would be a very good way to make life easier.

A Test of Humility

- Do I overcome my resistance to act when there is a risk of looking bad?

- Do I feel secure and satisfied with who I am?

- Am I transparent, spontaneous, and open, presenting myself to others as I truly am?

- Do I have a tendency to think the best of others to avoid living in an atmosphere of suspicion and doubt?

- Do I acknowledge my mistakes with simplicity and clarity?

- If I have gifts or exceptional talents in a specific area, do I use them with humility, avoiding ostentation and pretension?

- Do I systematically reject doing things based on what everyone else thinks?

25. OPENNESS

Trusting Yourself to Others

Openness to others is an act of humility. It means recognizing we cannot go very far if we go it alone. It is also a form of prudence. It does not take a sharp mind to realize that humanity survives by virtue of a fine network of relationships woven from mutual needs.

Openness to others means recognizing our need to rely on others. First and foremost, we need God. We are the work of his hands and the breath of his spirit (see Genesis 2:7). Without God's act of creation, we would not exist. In fact, this divine act of pure love embraces and sustains every moment of our lives. Humanity, always adolescent, has tried many times throughout history to free itself from this radical dependency. The more we deny our relationship with God, the more exposed and alone we feel. Henri de Lubac, a French theologian, described this situation in a book suggestively titled *The Drama of Atheist Humanism*.

Fortunately, many people today remember to say "God willing..." or "Heaven help us...." These are phrases of great realism. They reveal the conviction that we are in God's hands more than in our own.

Opening ourselves up to God requires turning to him at every moment, in big things and small. He is the only one who knows the big picture of our life. Not only that, he alone knows the plan that justifies our existence. How could we not ask for guidance and direction to fulfill it? Even in the smallest decisions of everyday life, you can tell who is connected to God and who is not.

I know a singer-songwriter of extraordinary talent. Before sitting down to compose, he pauses for silence and prayer. In this way, he finds inspiration and motivation for his work. There cannot be a more inspiring muse than God himself, who is the owner, Lord, and author of authentic beauty.

Next in order, we must open ourselves up to our family. Among mammals, the human infant is the most unable to fend for his- or herself. If abandoned, the baby would perish. This is not a flaw in nature. It is proof that human beings need deeper, tighter, and more enduring interpersonal ties than do those in the rest of the animal kingdom.

"The Lord God said: It is not good for the man to be alone" (Genesis 2:18). Humans need to live with others, and family is the closest and most welcoming community possible for a human being. Unfortunately, life's fast pace and the countless distractions that find a way into our homes are distancing and disintegrating many families. We must reclaim the true home, the place where parents and children gather, perhaps not around a literal fireplace, but around a figurative fire of love, affection, and interest in each other. Only in this way can we go beyond our selfish tendency toward isolation and self-reliance.

As a child, I always enjoyed it when there were people around, there were lights on in the house, and there was also human warmth. I felt sad the few times I stayed home alone. It seemed like an abandoned nest. Once, I left home without permission to play at a neighbor's house. A couple of hours later, I came back and found no one at home. There was only a little note stuck to the fridge that said, "Kiko (my childhood nickname): We went to the movies with all your brothers and sisters. Mom and Dad." That was one of the worst punishments I ever received.

Living together with our family demands dedicating time to give and receive, speak and listen, embrace and forgive, share words of affection, pay attention to details, help, and give lots of hugs and kisses. I know of a religious group that practices a very interesting family activity. They call it "Family Night." Each family picks a night of the week. Nobody takes on any other commitments that night. The family gets together that evening in their living room to read and freely comment on a part of the Gospel. Afterward, they share some activity that helps build family unity. There are many different ones, but all aim at getting to know each other better, improving relationships and communication, and so forth. There is also a moment of prayer, usually centered on giving thanks. The night concludes with a simple and delicious family dinner in an almost festive atmosphere. Initiatives such as this one can change a family's dynamics and give it an indestructible unity. Fr. Patrick Peyton's saying is true: "The family that prays together stays together."

Friendship is another form of openness to others that is necessary to conquer self-sufficiency. A friend is someone whom we can trust and turn to for support. We see ourselves in them, and we can share our most intimate thoughts and feelings with them. A friend is a companion, confidant, and advisor. A friend is an ally of our humility and willing to tell us what we need to hear even if it's not pleasant. Friendship expresses a particular kind of emotional openness. For this reason, it is able to defy time, difficulties, and even momentary estrangements.

When I was in medical school, I used to brag about the knowledge I acquired as a teenager doing first-response work for the Red Cross, particularly reading electrocardiograms. From the age of fifteen, I knew how to interpret the graph following Dubin's method: rate, rhythm, axis, hypertrophy, and infarction. I yearned for opportunities to show off my knowledge. Finally, the day arrived when we were going to be taught how to place the electrodes on a patient's chest. Obviously, I jumped ahead of the technician reciting the order in which to place the electrodes: "white, black, brown, green, red...." One of my best friends interrupted me with curt words that helped me immensely: "We know you know it all," he said with irony. "Now let the rest of us learn."

Friendship normally develops in concentric circles, from the most intimate to the most distant. A sound way to cultivate friendship is to choose a good circle of friends with whom to keep in touch habitually, perhaps on a weekly or monthly basis. It is even more important to know when to seek out a good friend to share personal situations or difficulties, listen to that friend's advice and receive encouragement and understanding.

Friendship often requires a challenging virtue: obedience. The word comes from the Latin *ob-audiere,* which means "to listen to." In its strictest sense, obedience is to submit to a higher authority. There is also room for an "obedience of equals," which means listening to and obeying those who love us, even if they do not have authority over us. A brother and a friend always have the right to get into our business without any authorization other than their concerned and sincere love.

In this way, we circumvent the grave danger of subjectivity, looking at situations based solely on our limited point of view and making too many unilateral decisions. Those who depend exclusively on their personal judgment are relying on an awful advisor, because no one is a good judge of his own cause. A friend sees from angles and perspectives that we do not. The eyes of a good friend help us see more and see better, becoming for us a window to objectivity.

Listening to a friend is also a way of freeing ourselves from the power of momentary whims. There is a well-known passage from the *Odyssey* in which Homer's hero, Odysseus, orders his sailors to tie him to the mast so he won't give in to the seductive song of the sirens. His friends obey him, and thanks to that drastic measure, Odysseus could resist the temptation to throw himself into the sea and swim toward the fearful sirens. Sometimes, our good friends must also tie us up at times to keep us from succumbing to danger.

Test of Openness

- Do I frequently consider the fact that I am more in God's hands than in my own?

- Do I habitually pray to God for light, guidance, and strength?

- Do I value the lessons I am taught by my family?

- Do I enjoy the time I spend sharing with my family or do I find excuses to isolate myself and spend time alone?

- Am I humble, allowing others to counsel me?

- Do I choose my friends well? Do I allow them to tell it like it is?

- Do I appreciate teamwork?

26. Detachment From Self

How to Heal a Swollen Ego

As we saw before, swollen egos suffer from hypersensitivity. Any disregard offends and hurts them. As the ego shrinks, one feels relief, relaxation, and greater tolerance to slights.

To set the ego aside to avoid suffering could seem absurd, something like stripping oneself of skin not to feel cold. It is, however, what our ego needs to be disregarded a bit. This toughens its skin, adapts it, and even leaves it armored for future blows in life.

The first way to shrink the ego is to learn to forget. It's often said that to be happy one needs good health and a poor memory. Many people torment themselves for years by remembering time and time again harm done to them, either real or imaginary. It's a masochistic way of bringing back the past and making the injury endure. Licking your wounds slows down the healing process.

It's true that there are blows in life we can't ignore or bury into oblivion. To ignore them completely could even be damaging. We must suffer through and cry over these blows to assimilate them, but that is different from dwelling on the pain to the point at which we start to enjoy it in a perverse way. We must flee from those situations. This is why it is utterly important to learn to manage our thoughts. It means developing the ability to focus selectively on a specific positive task, such as helping someone in need, reliving a happy memory, or even savoring the anticipated joy of an upcoming event. This selective focus, which is ultimately the result of a personal decision, is a resource that is always available. It only needs a bit of personal discipline.

Sometimes negative thoughts are very persistent, even obsessive. It becomes almost impossible to think about anything else. Such thoughts act like those annoying flies that can swarm around your head in certain climates. One must not attempt to eliminate such thoughts at all costs. It would be counterproductive. One must leave them in peace and not pay any attention to them. Let the insect fly around all it wants. One must keep focused on other things. Slowly, those thoughts start to lose strength and end up being drowned out by our other occupations.

Hypersensitivity also manifests itself by a tendency to connect dots too hastily and judge others' behavior. In this manner, we jump to negative conclusions that are more the result of wounded sensitivity than of healthy logic. The solution is objectivity. We need to avoid making hasty judgments or conjectures, supposing things that are not proven to be true, or allowing ourselves to delve into the impenetrable world of someone else's intentions. Trust evidence only. As long as we are not certain of the contrary, it is advisable to give others the benefit of the doubt. It is better for our mental health that we err by giving a person the benefit of the doubt rather than casting judgment. To be objective is to be reasonable, which implies rejecting the imagination's irrational impulses that often tend to overflow and destroy the peace.

The universe of interpersonal relationships is complex and unpredictable. It's impossible to never hurt anyone or to never be hurt by someone else. I, for one, have realized how I have left a trail of hurt and offended people in my wake, practically without even knowing it. In the same way, we are all potential victims of others' disregard in terms of lack of attention, insensitivity, or oversight. As if that is not bad enough, hypersensitivity blows it all out of proportion. It magnifies offenses, giving them more importance than they merit. This is why we must learn to tell our ego, "It's not that big a deal," and return time and again to an objective point of view to correct any distorted perspectives and to moderate our reactions.

There is another wise habit for combating hypersensitivity, which is not to feel entitled to any special treatment from others. A while back, a very generous family lent us their home in Valle de Bravo (a beautiful place in Mexico) to spend a restful weekend. The house was very well-organized and outfitted with ample means of entertainment and luxuries. While walking around the rooms to settle down, we found a sign on the wall with the three basic rules of the house. The one that most caught my attention said: "Feel right at home. Everything is at your disposal…but don't expect anyone to wait on you!"

Perhaps at times we expect too much from people, so it becomes easy to feel disappointed and even offended when they don't live up to those expectations. If we foster the expectation of being treated as we deserve, we'll always be a step away from feeling let down and getting upset. If we cultivate the idea that nobody owes us anything instead, we'll see everything as a gift. We won't feel hurt when we don't receive something we weren't expecting anyway.

Experience teaches us that in general the deepest wounds in life don't come from outsiders but rather from the intimate circle of those we love the most. A husband or wife, son or daughter, or sibling or friend can most hurt us, surely because we expect more care and consideration from them. Such wounds heal promptly, however, if we put our own rights aside and live with an attitude of giving without expecting anything in return. The more unattached our heart is, the more resilient. Actually, only such a heart can counter an offense with a loving and humble action. And no one can resist a heart of this kind.

Test of Detachment from Self

- Do I easily forget when I have been offended or hurt?

- When I feel offended, do I tell myself time and time again, "It wasn't that big a deal?"

- Do I believe that nobody owes me anything and so receive everything as a gift?

- When I run into someone who has hurt me, do I put my wounded self aside?

- Am I objective? Do I avoid reading into, interpreting, and judging other people's behaviors?

- Do I believe in all the good I hear and only believe the bad that I witness?

- Do I live for others without expecting anything in return?

27. AUTHENTICITY

Building the Real You

Socializing is a uniquely human phenomenon. Animals gather in herds, schools, hives, or packs, not in societies. Although animals might gather in groups for protection, human beings are the only truly social creatures. Being social implies conforming to customs, traditions, and rules of conduct according to the cultural context in which we live. This, in and of itself, is not bad. The purpose of society is not to cancel out a person's individuality but to meld individuals into a community that creates a better environment to live in and the ability to pass on history and traditions.

Not everything in our society today is commendable. In fact, ours has incorporated negative, even harmful, values that we have to fight against, but opposing everything about our modern culture is foolish. The aggressive slant of various countercultural movements that have emerged in the last decades is significant. Many of them rise up against the values of a Christian culture that has been the foundation of our Western civilization. In the name of secularism, they attempt to institute an amoral culture, a culture that ignores those values they feel have been implemented by religious faith alone, when in fact many of those values have been legitimized by reason and experience through centuries of social learning. These values coincide, in good measure, with the virtues pointed out in this book.

Let's look again at the rebel without a cause, the eccentric and original naysayer of every conversation. This rebelliousness, as we examined, expresses a need to distinguish oneself by way of being different or contrary. Paradoxically, the antidote against this behavior is true authenticity, acting by personal conviction and not peer pressure, regardless of where that lands us in popular opinion.

Rebelliousness represents a false posture. Rebellious actions are determined by the behavior of others. If the majority choose "A," the rebel will choose "B." If the majority were to choose "B," however, the rebel would choose "A." Such rebellious decisions do not follow personal convictions but simply oppose the personal convictions of a majority. An authentic person does not fear conforming to a group when his or her personal conviction or taste aligns with it. An authentic person only opposes it when the group acts contrary to his or her fundamental values.

As with the other virtues, our best example can be found in Jesus Christ. He did not hesitate to mold himself to our world when, as St. Paul says, "he emptied himself, taking the form of a slave, coming in human likeness..." (Philippians 2:7). Coming as he did from celestial glory, we could not think of anyone more estranged from our world than him. Jesus adapted himself, however, to the Jewish culture of the time. He learned the language, mannerisms, traditions, and rituals. For many years, he was just another person in town until the time came for him to reveal himself and begin his mission.

In everyday life, an authentic person is a simple, humble person who likes to go unnoticed. This person does not contrive eccentricities to stand out from the crowd but embraces those things that give life joy and meaning. This person would rather be a contributor than a detractor and prefers building unity to creating division. An authentic person is a team player and has no problem with being part of something bigger than him- or herself.

The authentic person is flexible, adapting easily to people, times, and circumstances. Being around such a person is a joy. In conversation, such an individual's usual response to someone else's opinion is encouragement and compromise, even if he or she disagrees.

Along the same lines, people who are authentic are not afraid to express their point of view, even if it is different and unique. They are not chameleons that change color according to the group that surrounds them. They assert and propose opinions and ideas when appropriate, and even complaints when justified. In this sense, authenticity is fundamental to personal communication. Where there is a lack of authenticity, there is poor communication.

Authenticity demands maturity. Only those who are mature are capable of accepting themselves and their circumstances without hesitation. The mature can accept themselves as they are and accept that they are part of a greater community. Authentic persons know they must assume a constructive role in society, a society which they both need and is needed by others. Only mature persons acknowledge that deep down they are not so different from everyone else.

Authentic individuals see society as an open stage on which a myriad of styles, proposals, perspectives, and values—perhaps unlike theirs—are all given equal time and attention. They are willing to learn from others as well as contribute.

If rebelliousness divides, then authenticity unites. Perhaps the greatest dilemma in today's world stems from two inauthentic postures: ethnic, cultural, or religious extremism on one hand, and superficial homogeneity on the other. The virtue of authenticity could be the touchstone, in terms of firmness and flexibility, for resolving this apparent dilemma and making the world what it should be: a real family of nations.

Test of Authenticity

- Do I act in a way that is natural to who I am, rather than one that draws attention to me as an individual?

- Do I accept social conventions that are not harmful or fundamentally bad?

- Is my behavior prompted by my values and convictions or by a need to be different?

- Have I learned the art of dialogue? Do I listen more than I talk?

- Do I get my hands dirty when supporting a good cause?

- Am I authentic in all circumstances? Or am I a chameleon who changes values depending on popular opinion?

- Am I open and respectful of the principles and values of others?

28. A LIFE PLAN

Let's Get to Work

We have finally arrived at the decisive chapter. Having gone through the primary vices and virtues, it is time to develop a sound life plan as the result of this knowledge.

To achieve this, we must use what we have learned to diagnose ourselves:

- Which vice is most prevalent in my life?
- Which vice is the most problematic?

Once this is established, we must ask ourselves:

- In what way does this vice affect my personal life?
- How frequently does this vice intrude on my life?
- How does it alter my relationships with others?
- How does it affect my professional life?
- Where will this behavior lead me at the end of my life?

If our dominant flaw is causing these kinds of problems, we must do something about it. The goal of having a life plan is just that, to establish concrete objectives to limit the damage our vice can do and to use our struggle against that flaw to develop a virtuous, mature, and full personality.

In fact, explicitly or implicitly, most of us follow some form of plan for work, school, physical exercise, and even social activities. Life demands it. The most relevant plan in our lives should be our life plan. This plan defines who and how we are and who and how we ought to be.

"Who I am" should be clearer to you now after having taken a detailed look at the most common vices. "Who I ought to be" should be clearer as well after learning the principal virtues. It is now a matter of transforming the tension between "who we are" and "who we ought to be" into a road map or step-by-step instructions that help us set out in the right direction. This is our life plan.

There are various life plan models. Each one has its positives and negatives. The following is a model that I have used with some success, but feel free to modify it to your personal needs. The process begins, as previously noted, with the diagnosis of our dominant flaw. You may find it helpful to go back and review chapter sixteen on the dominant flaw to remember how to diagnose it. Once your dominant flaw has been diagnosed, you can develop your life plan, using this outline as your guide:

1. Ideal
2. Personal motto
3. Obstacle
4. Resources
5. Action plan

1. The "ideal" of our life plan will always be Jesus Christ. He who is God incarnate did not only take on our nature to save us but also to give us a model to which to aspire. Imitating Christ is the shortest route to growing and maturing as people. Therefore, he is the ideal to follow and imitate in any life plan. To focus our plan further, we must give Jesus Christ a last name. This will be the aspect or virtue in his personality that we need the most to combat our dominant flaw. If, for example, your dominant flaw is laziness, your ideal could be "Jesus Christ, tireless apostle." If your dominant flaw is pride, your ideal could be "Jesus Christ, gentle and humble of heart."

2. The plan's "personal motto" is a slogan for our life. It consists of a simple, motivational phrase that has the dual purpose of reminding and encouraging us to keep in line with our plan. It is best to create your own personal motto given your individual personality and sensibilities. Examples of such phrases are:

- "You can do it, keep going!"
- "With love, I can face anything!"
- "I choose to be free!"

If you prefer, your motto could be a short prayer instead, such as: "Make my heart like yours!"

3. The "obstacle" is our dominant flaw and its manifestations. It is important to incorporate our flaw into our life plan. There is no worse enemy than that which we refuse to acknowledge. It is vital to break this vice down into its two or three most common manifestations in our life.

For example, if your dominant flaw is pride, you should point out specific prideful behaviors:

- I'm impatient with my spouse.
- I'm arrogant with my employees.
- I silently criticize others.

If your dominant flaw is laziness, you might point out:

- I do not get up right away.
- I postpone difficult tasks.
- I waste too much time watching television.

This breakdown of our dominant flaw with its concrete manifestations is key when making our plan of action. If we don't admit how our dominant flaw influences our life, we won't be able to stop it.

4. Our "resources" are prayer and sacrifice. We talk about resources because we cannot be successful in our life plan all on our own. These particular resources are, in fact, the two greatest ways Christ gave us to conquer moral failures: "Watch and pray that you may not undergo the test. The spirit is willing, but the flesh is weak" (Matthew 26:41). Pray and ask God to give you a hand by sharing his grace, without which we cannot go far. Sacrifice means doing our part by being vigilant, avoiding dangerous situations, overcoming temptations, and fighting against our dominant flaw, even if that means stepping outside our comfort zone or giving up a habitual indulgence.

Prayer does not mean making a list of specific ways we need God to help us. (God knows better than we do what we need.) Instead, it means constantly asking God for his grace to conquer our dominant flaw in whatever way he shares it with us. Sacrifice, in turn, does not mean turning to special penances or grand gestures of sacrifice that have nothing to do with our dominant flaw. Our greatest sacrifice will be to fight against that flaw with virtuous attitudes and behaviors in small ways, every day.

5. The "action plan" consists of two or three virtuous attitudes and behaviors we can use to fight our dominant flaw. Determining those points will be simple. All you have to do is focus on the concrete manifestations of your dominant flaw, which you should already have listed in your "obstacle" section, and write the opposite attitude or action. If you get stuck, think "what would Jesus do" or how would Christ respond. For example, if our vice is pride, using the previously noted manifestations, our plan of action could be:

- I will be particularly patient with my spouse.
- I will treat my employees with special consideration.
- I will think well of others, noting their virtues more so than their flaws.

Or if we are lazy:

- I will get up as soon as the alarm clock goes off.
- I will have a well-defined, daily to-do list that I will take care of in order of importance, not of ease.
- I will dedicate more time to productive tasks, including rest, and less time to watching television.

You should keep the tone positive. It may feel like you are just giving up something you enjoy or giving in to people who are difficult, but in reality you are transforming those situations to leave them open to an even greater good.

A well-developed life plan is in itself a very brief document. The easier it looks on paper, the easier it will be to start putting it into action. Plans that have too many points or are too complex end up being ineffective. A life plan's effectiveness truly resides in its simplicity. We have to be realistic about what we can accomplish, especially if this is the first time tackling our vices head-on.

Finally, it is beneficial to put our plan through a trial by fire to determine whether or not it's ready to go. This trial consists of just one question. Will our action plan be difficult to integrate into our daily life? If the answer is yes, we can safely say our plan is well crafted and that we have been honest about our flaws. If, on the other hand, the answer is no and the plan will be easy and comfortable to implement, we should consider reassessing our dominant flaw and redrafting our plan.

29. THE VITAL TEN

A Supportive Environment
for a Virtuous Life

Virtues do not bloom in barren soil. They require a favorable context and climate. We can create this climate through a balanced, full, and disciplined life. Therefore, as the culmination of this brief exposition on vices and virtues, I would like to offer a model of ten activities or pursuits to engage in over the course of a week. This model leads to a wholesome and harmonious life, the ideal climate for virtue. I call this set of activities the "vital ten."

To put the vital ten into action, consider the scope of a week. It's a period of time ample enough for all of our activities, but not so lengthy that it is easy to lose track or be too intimidated to start. A week has its own rhythm, a recurrence of days that orients us in time and makes it easy to create a routine.

A week has 168 hours. This is important. These hours become our budget of time for the vital ten. The idea is not to carry out these ten activities as quickly as possible and then dedicate the rest of our time to doing nothing (or falling back into our dominant flaw). The vital ten includes space for downtime and relaxation according to an alternating pattern of activities, some that may tire us and others that should renew us. But these vital ten should fill all 168 hours.

The vital ten is a full meal consisting of three main courses and dessert. Each entree, in turn, includes three ingredients or activities.

The first entree is that of survival. This is the most fundamental and essential of the ten because it deals with our physical, mental, and spiritual renewal. Its elements are:

- Prayer
- Nourishment
- Sleep

Prayer is, in a general sense, speaking with God. We each choose how much time in our day is dedicated to God. Many limit themselves to a weekly form of worship, such as going to Mass on Sunday. They give God one hour and leave 167 to the remaining activities. Others may already be more aware that it is not God who needs them for one hour a week, but they who are in need of God, all the time! As a result, in addition to the mandatory weekly worship, they pray, meditate, practice personal devotions, read spiritual books, and more. It is a great way to build up strength, inspiration, light, and guidance for the journey.

Nourishment (or what we eat) is the second activity for survival. Nutritionists and doctors insist that we need at least three main meals per day (breakfast, lunch, dinner), perhaps including a snack between meals. The objective is to maintain the necessary level of physical energy to work, study, deal with difficulties, dialogue, play, socialize, and rest to the best of our abilities. When our energy level drops, we feel weaker, become easily distracted, and can be irritable with others and vulnerable to our vices. Meals not only supply us with physical energy but also provide very important breaks that give each day the structure and space to share time with family and friends.

The third ingredient for survival is sleep. Science alerts us more every day to the importance of sleep. Nothing is more restorative to our nervous system than getting enough sleep and sleeping well. The average adult requires between six and eight hours of sleep per day. Given the biological rhythms of sleep, it is necessary to sleep without interruptions so those sleep cycles can run their natural course. If it's possible, try to create a nighttime routine to set yourself up for the best possible rest. Some things to consider include:

- Eating a light supper
- Setting aside work or stressors several hours before bed
- Avoiding strenuous exercise late in the evening
- Going without television or internet in the bedroom
- Having set bedtimes and wake-up times

This may seem idealistic or even impossible, especially given life's hectic and demanding pace. Still, it's worth a try. It's worth keeping in mind that being well rested is not just for ourselves, but can actually be a service to others. Being well rested keeps us calm, patient, having a good attitude, and in a better mood.

Our second entree is personal responsibilities:

- Work and/or study
- Physical exercise
- Reading

Work and/or study are essential if we are to be responsible members of our family and of society. As we talked about earlier with the parable of the talents, we are all called to use and multiply the gifts God has given us. The kind of work and/or study that figures into our life depends on our vocation, but none of us is exempt from the requirement to be productive in some form or another and to provide for our own needs and those of others.

When talking about our work, whatever form that takes, we must remember the principle of "all things in moderation." Students, as well as professionals, must remember it is the quality of our work, not the time we put into it, that really counts. It is easy to get caught up in the mindset that we must devote all our time and energy to work and/or school, and although it is important to put our best efforts into everything we do, focusing exclusively on this one aspect of our life can lead to vices. Beyond this, we can find ourselves in a downward spiral of tiredness and stress, which will result in poor performance, chronic fatigue, and even depression. It is preferable to study and/or work with focus and effort during an assigned period of time, followed by intervals of time set aside for family life and rest, than it is to work at a less intense pace continuously and indefinitely.

Physical exercise is the second ingredient of personal responsibilities. It is an essential activity not only for physical health but also for emotional and moral stability. Mens sana in corpore sano ("a healthy mind in a healthy body"), as the Latin proverb advises. The recommended amount of physical activity for adults is thirty minutes per day or its equivalent spread out over at least two sessions a week. The exercise referred to here is the aerobic-cardiovascular type. It must be demanding but not exhausting. People must evaluate, with a doctor's advice, the most appropriate type of exercise according to their age and health.

Sports medicine has proven that after thirty minutes of good exercise, our body secretes endorphins that flow into our bloodstream. Endorphins are molecules that generate a feeling of relaxation as well as physical and mental well-being. This discharge of endorphins can be an unparalleled antidote to stress. This is perhaps why some doctors say physical exercise is the best psychiatrist. It not only releases tension but also helps us avoid dangerous methods of escaping from stress such as alcohol, drugs, or other morally compromising activities.

Reading weekly can be very enriching, specifically reading that adds to our general knowledge in literature, history, arts, sciences, and so forth. It is advisable to set aside a couple of hours a week for this kind of learning. Classical literature by time-honored authors (for example, Homer, Horatius, Euripides, Shakespeare) as well as more modern ones (G.K. Chesterton, C.S. Lewis, and many others) can be particularly fruitful. In addition to being entertaining, literature offers us a wealth of wisdom and knowledge about the human heart, life, and even our professional life. Other than literature, it can be helpful to read nonfiction books that enhance our spiritual life (like this one!) or news reports and world events that keep us up to date on what's going on around us.

The third and last main entree refers to other people:

- Our family
- Our friends
- Our community

First and foremost, we have our family: our spouse, children, and extended family. Family life entails many different ways of spending time together, such as engaging in conversation, resolving conflicts, relaxing, and sharing intimacy. It is imperative to dedicate time to building and rebuilding this vital space. In addition to daily family life and special moments of quality time, it's good to take advantage of weekends, or days off if you do not work a traditional work week, to enjoy a more relaxed and easygoing space. Going out as a family to eat, to the movies, to go shopping, or engaging in any other family friendly activities provides opportunities for recreating connections, strengthening bonds, and enjoying our family's affection.

DIAGRAM OF THE VITAL TEN

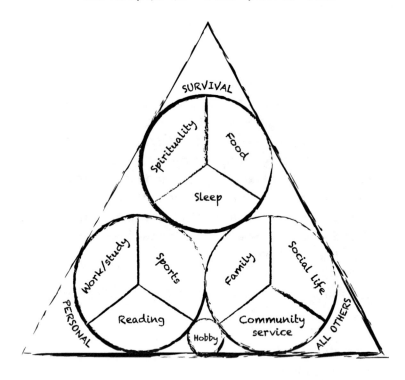

Second, we have friends who make up our social life. This includes social engagements and activities of all kinds, from baptisms, first communions, or weddings, to informal weekly gatherings of friends sharing a hobby, activity, or just time together. Wholesome gatherings of any kind favor openness, relaxation, and variety while strengthening the bonds of our friendships.

Finally, we have the time we must dedicate to community. Many cultures are very focused on community service. It is almost imperative to devote some time to others through social work, service, or ministry. The needs of a community are broad and varied. We can each choose how to give to others according to our ability and availability. This refers not so much to our money but to our time and effort. The fruits of such labor do not just benefit the community. The giver is also nourished by the experience.

At the end of this meal comes the final course, dessert. Once all nine of the previous activities have been covered, we have space for an activity of pure personal delight, a hobby. Hobbies allow us to follow our passions, give us something to look forward to, entertain us, and give us some distraction from daily stresses. A suggested hobby (if you don't already have one) would be to take up a musical instrument. As soon as you overcome the initial difficulties of learning, the instrument becomes a friend and longed-for refuge. Those who have no inclination toward music could try the visual arts, such as painting, sculpture, ceramics, and crafts of various genres. These hobbies have the tremendous advantage of actively involving you in creation and capturing your attention with something unique, creative, and gratifying. There are countless other hobbies and forms of entertainment as well: watching or playing sports, analyzing movies, listening to music, going to the theater, visiting museums, and more. The important thing is to have at least one hobby and cultivate it until it becomes a passion.

The vital ten is not a rigid structure. Unforeseen situations frequently arise and get in the way of our orderly plan. Rather than being a rigid necessity for a virtuous life, the vital ten provide a guideline that points us in the right direction, toward important activities in our daily life and away from those that lead us into our vices. All ten are important, because habitually neglecting any one of them will, sooner or later, have negative consequences for our physical, emotional, mental, or spiritual life, as well as affect our marriage, family, or social relationships. Consistent attention to the vital ten is usually accompanied by a sense of satisfaction rooted in a demanding, productive, and fulfilled life.

THE VITAL TEN

ACTIVITY	SUGGESTED HOURS (PER WEEK)
Activity	3-5
Food	14
Sleep/ personal hygiene	60
Work/study	40
Sports	4-7
Reading	2-3
Family	26
Social life	3-5
Community service	2-3
Hobby	3-5
TOTAL	168

Conclusion

Someone once said that life is not the party we all wish for, but while we are here we have no option but to dance. Perhaps this book has been an opportunity for you to pause for a moment, review your style, and learn new steps.

We now know ourselves better, with more objectivity and maturity. We accept ourselves with more serenity and humility and are on our way to improving ourselves through a life plan. It is possible that from now on our life may march to the beat of a different drum. The only constant in life is change.

Our primary obstacle? Our own resistance to that change. Our own selfishness is and will always be like a stubborn old man who insists on following his old ways. If we yield to God, however, we will change and, at least in certain areas of our life, a new person will be revealed. Everyone will appreciate it. Our family, friends, coworkers, even our own heart, will live more peacefully.

As the psalmist prayed, "Lord, let me know my end, the number of my days, that I may learn how frail I am" (Psalm 39:5). Time is fleeting. It is urgent to get to work. Each day is a new and unique opportunity to work on changing ourselves. In the moment it takes us to have a thought, desire, or make a decision, we must fight the great battle of virtue against vice. This is what it means to take life seriously.

Undoubtedly, there will be failures and losses, but do not be discouraged. Success lies in starting over when we have failed. I once read that there are two types of human beings: the ones who stay down after they have fallen, lamenting their fate, and those who get up, pick up the pieces, and continue living.

To overcome our flaws, grow, and mature, we must start over a thousand and one times. In order to be human, with the array of contradictions that we carry within, starting over isn't only the right path. It's the only path.

CPSIA information can be obtained at www.ICGtesting.com
Printed in the USA
LVOW10s1509040516

486574LV00054BA/1014/P